ROBBYN MACDONALD'S

— *Exquisite* —

EMBROIDERY

The Five Mile Press

——— *Dedication* ———

In memory of my grandmother, Janet Mason,
and her beautiful garden.

The Five Mile Press

The Five Mile Press Pty Ltd
22 Summit Road Noble Park Victoria 3174 Australia

First published 1996

Text © Robbyn Macdonald
Illustrations © The Five Mile Press Pty Ltd
Design © The Five Mile Press Pty Ltd
All rights reserved

Editor: Barbara Whiter
Design and Production: Emma Borghesi
Photography: Neil Lorimer
Illustrations: Bryony Dade

Printed in Hong Kong by Toppan Printing Co.

National Library of Australia Cataloguing-in-Publication data:

Macdonald, Robbyn
Robbyn Macdonald's Exquisite Embroidery
ISBN 0 86788 443 6
1. Embroidery — Patterns. I. Title. II. Exquisite Embroidery.

746.44041

Contents

Potpourri Friendship Quilt: This quilt was born from an idea to incorporate some of my students' embroidery, whose skills range from beginner to experienced embroiderer, into my book. See page 96.

Introduction

*E*mbroidery is the term describing how a piece of fabric is decorated by sewing. This can be done either simply with coloured cotton, silk or wool threads, or by the more elaborate use of beautiful ribbons, beads, gold and silver threads.

Embroidery in the nineteenth century was extremely popular, as indeed it is today, and it was an important part of life for most upper- and middle-class ladies. Materials used then were of much the same nature as today — including cotton, wool, silk, linen and the more elaborate and finely woven taffetas, brocades, velvets and shiny satins.

Embroidery threads were of a similar nature too. They ranged from plain coloured cottons and wools to the glossy silk floss and chenille threads such as those we use today. Ribbon embroidery was also popular and was worked in beautifully coloured narrow silk ribbon.

In the past, some of the more unusual materials used were fish scales, feathers from swansdown, guinea fowl, pheasants and peacocks, iridescent beetle wings from India and dried husks of larva cases. Although materials used today differ somewhat from these last examples, the idea is always the same — to create a beautiful and lasting piece of embroidery.

I love to create new embroidery pieces and my formal dining room becomes transformed into a mass of the tools of my trade. I have to admit that I work in the midst of chaos with all manner of fabrics, ribbons, threads and braids piled on my dining table and spilling on to the floor. My carpet sparkles with fallen glitter and beads, but this delightful chaos gives me such inspiration.

It is so exciting matching materials and ribbons and watching your piece come together.

Embroidery does not have to be perfect — in fact, it is better if it isn't — nature after all isn't and no two flowers are ever the same. Individuality is important and the pleasure is gained from producing your own original piece of art. For instance, my youngest son's school uniform pocket was in need of a stitch and I embroidered a beetle to hold it up — I just can't help myself! My husband quickly mastered the art of sewing on a shirt button!

So a word of caution, once you start to dabble in the world of ribbon embroidery, it won't be long before you too, like so many before you, are hooked by its charm. You begin slowly with a few interesting ribbons, threads and a piece of calico, but before long you end up with a dining room like mine! Happy embroidering!!

ROBBYN MACDONALD

Materials, Handy Hints & Framing

Fabrics

There is an abundance of fabrics to choose from today, but one area that I feel is overlooked in the craft area is the use of bridal fabrics. I have used a wide variety of bridal fabrics throughout this book and not only are they beautiful to work with, today the selection of colours and textures is simply stunning. Bridal fabrics and trimmings always add a luxurious quality to embroideries and they should not be considered purely for weddings.

Stencilled Cushions and Embroidery

I have always loved to paint and, over the years since I began embroidery, I have tried to combine the two in different ways. Using fabric paints and any material from calico through to fine silks as your canvas, you can achieve some beautiful results and a decorative base for your embroideries.

A very quick, easy, and effective way to paint a design on fabric is to use a stencil. There is such a fantastic variety of stencils available now and whether you choose a simple or elaborate design, the technique of application is so easy.

Stencils are fun to use and can lead to very interesting creations of embroidery as the stencil pattern can help in deciding your embroidery design. For instance, the rambling ivy leaves I have used in the Buttercup Ivy cushion project create a base for roses and grapes and suits a more elongated cushion. However, the Formal Glory bolster has a more formal stencil which lends itself for use as either a border on a square cushion or, as I have shown, one which can be effectively used on each end of a bolster. So don't be afraid to combine fabric paint and material, as you will be delighted with the results you can achieve.

Handy Hints

There are a few helpful tips to note that will make embroidery less difficult. Firstly the needle size and type can be crucial depending on the stitches you are working. It is important to have a packet of assorted size chenille needles on hand — I use sizes 18/24. These are great when using pure silk ribbons, and for threading the wide ribbons usually used for reverse ribbon leaves and large ribbon buds.

A large eye is needed to take the ribbon width and to pull through the material. If the material you are using is a tightly woven weave, then a stiletto is essential. Just punch a hole where you wish to bring your needle through and it will glide smoothly. Embroidery is after all, a relaxing pastime, and with a stiletto handy, believe me, it will be!

Assorted crewel needles size 3/9 are good to use for all other thread work with one exception — the bullion stitch, for which I use a long straw needle with the largest eye possible. Straw needles usually have extremely small eyes and are very tedious to thread but if you use one of the larger ones your bullion stitches will be much easier to tackle.

When making ribbon roses I sometimes combine two ribbons to achieve a shadowy effect. You do this by laying the ribbons together, and using as one. This is particularly attractive when you combine an organdy ribbon with a solid colour — you achieve both colours and textures through the folds of your rose. Try experimenting with different types and colours of ribbon and you will be delighted by the outcome.

One thread I enjoy using is floss. It gives a lovely sheen to your embroidery and adds a gloss to cotton thread work. When using floss a simple trick is to dampen the length before beginning as this will prevent the yarn from twisting and knotting, and also helps to keep it from splitting.

Use of Templates

Twelve projects in this book have templates supplied (there are two for the Mademoiselle Piano Stool project). Depending upon your level of skill, you can use these as visual guides or actually transfer the patterns on to your fabric using tracing paper and a transfer pencil readily obtainable at art and craft stores.

Most templates have been reduced to 50% of the actual size to enable them to be included in the book; but all are captioned so there is no guessing as to reduction factors required. It is of course up to the individual embroiderer to decide what size to use the template: for example, if a smaller cushion is desired, keep the templates at 50% of the original size.

Framing

So many different effects can be achieved by framing and I think framing can really make or break the look of an embroidery. It is therefore important to take time in choosing the appropriate frame for your piece, and fortunately today there is an abundance of frames available.

Even before you get to the choice of a frame, there are many ways to enhance your embroidery. For instance, a clever framer can cover a matt board in the exact material you have used for your embroidery. This requires a skilful framer as they have to make certain no ripples of material appear. My framer has used this technique on the Cameo Cherub project using a pale pink matt board first and covering the outer board in the turquoise material I have used under the gold silk. Before my piece was framed I decorated the corners with lace and bows to give the embroidery a new dimension.

Another idea is to choose a plain frame, as I have done with the Crystal Iceberg project, and decorate it yourself. For this particular project, I painted some soft flowers and glued crystal buttons and beads, which matched those used in the embroidery itself, to the frame to create an original piece. Hunting through antique and bric-a-brac shops can bring some interesting and inexpensive discoveries. I found the wrought iron frame used on Sweet Pea Fairy Dreams in an antique shop. It housed a convex mirror and was in a very bad repair. I removed the mirror, cleaned and gilded the frame and then added some glitter to match my embroidery, and the result was an original and relatively inexpensive frame. My framer then put convex Perspex (convex glass is very difficult to find) in the frame and gave it a totally new look!

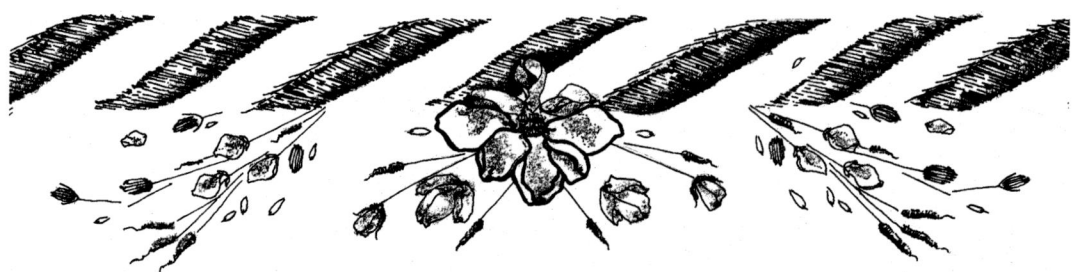

Above: template for Mademoiselle Piano Stool border which repeats, at 57%. Instructions begin opposite.

Mademoiselle Piano Stool

I bought this charming French piano stool at an auction — it was in good repair except for the very worn upholstery. To replace this I chose a heavy cream damask for several reasons: it is a robust fabric that is perfect for upholstery use; it can take the heaviness of the large embroidered ribbon roses and won't pucker; and it has a lovely self-pattern that sets the embroidery off nicely.

The embroidery design I created reproduced the decorative roses on the frame in a central embroidery and I embroidered a simple edging in satin stitch and small buds.

Materials

- 1 m heavy upholstery damask
- piano stool
- 3 m cream wire-edged ribbon, 25 mm wide
- 2 m cream double-sided satin ribbon, 25 mm wide
- 3 m Mokuba 4597 col. 14 (gold stripe), 15 mm wide
- 4 m pure silk ribbon col. 35 (gold), 7 mm wide
- 3 m pure silk ribbon col. 156 (cream), 4 mm wide
- gold Glista thread
- 3 m pure silk ribbon col. 56 (lime green), 4 mm wide
- 3 m double-sided satin ribbon (cream), 4 mm wide
- DMC Perle (pale green)
- 1 m Mokuba 4617 col. 7 (gold metallic), 15 mm wide
- cream Madeira floss
- DMC 842 (beige) (for bullion stitches)
- DMC 3013 (pale green) (for stems on all flowers)
- 1 m Mokuba 4599 col. 9 (murky green), 15 mm wide
- DMC Perle (cream)
- 0.25 m cream stripe ribbon with gold edges
- Mokuba braid 9212 col. 00 (cream) (small piece for centre of bow)

Method

1   Cut material size to suit your stool.

2   Make three iceberg roses using cream wire-edged and cream double-sided satin ribbon joined together for central part of rose. (See *Techniques and Stitch Glossary* to find how to make an iceberg rose.) Sew roses to centre of material. And, using Mokuba gold-striped ribbon, embroider lazy daisy leaves around the iceberg roses.

3   Embroider four ribbon daisies using gold pure silk, and two ribbon daisies using cream pure silk ribbons (ribbon daisies are created by embroidering three or four silk ribbon buds together). Use gold Glista thread to embroider two small bullions in centre of daisies and embroider two lazy daisy leaves at the base of each daisy using narrow lime green pure silk ribbon.

4   Using narrow cream doubled-sided satin ribbon, embroider seven ribbon buds where shown on template and embroider lime green pure silk ribbon lazy daisy leaves on either side of the buds. Embroider stems with one strand DMC Perle in pale green.

5   Using gold pure silk ribbon, embroider seven more ribbon buds. Then, with cream pure silk ribbon, create lazy daisy stitches either side, where shown on the template. Embroider lime green silk ribbon lazy daisy leaves either side of these buds. Again, embroider stems with one strand pale green DMC Perle thread.

6   Embroider three reverse ribbon leaves in gold metallic ribbon where shown on the template. Then embroider two cream floss straight stitch buds at each end of design. Using the DMC Perle pale green thread, fly stitch stems. Follow by embroidering beige DMC bullion buds where shown using three strands of the thread; use one strand pale green DMC for the stems. Embroider large lazy daisy leaves and reverse ribbon leaves around design using gold-striped ribbon and murky green rayon ribbon.

7   Work satin stitch ribbon shape on central roses and around stool using DMC Perle cream thread. Embroider tiny buds in cream pure silk and half daisies using pure silk gold throughout satin stitch edging as shown. Then embroider gold Glista bullion stitches using gold fly stitches to attach to large central half daisy at top of stool. Embroider beige DMC bullions using three strands throughout ribbon shape, then embroider cream floss straight stitch buds close to bullions as shown throughout ribbon shape.

8   Make two loops with gold-edged ribbon and sew in place to form a bow. Use a small piece of the Mokuba cream braid to highlight the centre of this bow. Using Perle thread in pale green embroider straight stitch stems on roses to finish stool and have a reputable upholsterer cover your heirloom.

Above: central template for Mademoiselle Piano Stool at 44%.

Above: template for central section of Souvenir de la Malmaison Rose cushion at 60%.

Souvenir de la Malmaison Rose

I find the most exciting aspect of embroidery is the sheer beauty of working with such glorious fabrics and ribbons. The inspiration gained from the colour, texture and pattern of both is never-ending and only limited by imagination.

This cushion with its bold, full-blown roses is not to be ignored and is reminiscent of a cushion you may find in a French ladies' boudoir.

Materials

- 0.5 m silk Herald Collection, rose colour plain silk for centre panel and back, cut 37 cm 30 cm (33 cm x 26 cm when sewn on fabric)
- piece 67 cm x 60 cm (60 cm x 44 cm when made up) silk Herald Collection, rose colour with tulip design (from quality fabric stores such as Lincraft: bridal section)
- 1 m Mokuba 4000 col. 65 (pink) (velvet cord)
- 3 old velvet leaves
- 2 m Mokuba 4647 crinkle ribbon col. 29 (dusky pink), 38 mm wide (for French roses)
- 1 m Mokuba 4647 crinkle ribbon col. 12 (cream), 38 mm wide (for French roses)
- 5 m Mokuba 4546 col. 29 (dusky pink), 25 mm wide (Scabiosa, fuchsias and ribbon roses)
- 3 m Mokuba 4546 col. 12 (cream), 25 mm wide (fuchsias and French rose)
- 2 m Mokuba 4570 col. 8 (pink silver-edged), 25 mm wide (ribbon rose and buds)
- 4 m Mokuba 4599 col. 9 (no-green), 15 mm wide (ribbon leaves)
- 2 m Mokuba 4597 col. 14 (gold-stripe organdy), 15 mm wide (ribbon leaves)
- DMC 778 (pink) — 3 strands for fuchsia stamens
- DMC 734 (green) — 1 strand for fuchsia stems
- DMC Perle 644 (pale green)
- 0.5 metre Mokuba 4586 col. 17 (lime green luminous), 25 mm (ribbon leaves)
- 2 m piping (covered in rose silk for the edges of the cushion)
- 4 tassels with cord attached

Method

1 Sew rose-coloured plain silk panel to tulip material either by hand or machine.

2 Hand stitch pink velvet cord around edge of this silk panel.

3 Stitch velvet leaves in position as shown in the photograph.

4 Make up three full blown French roses in the dusky pink and cream crinkle ribbons using directions in the *Techniques and Stitch Glossary*, and sew into place.

5 Make two ribbon roses combining dusky pink and pink silver-edged ribbon and stitch in place.

6 Make two Scabiosa flowers (using the instructions in the *Techniques and Stitch Glossary*) in the dusky pink ribbon mentioned in *Materials* — stitch in place as shown in the photograph.

7   Make three pink fuchsias and three cream fuchsias (again using the instructions contained within the *Techniques and Stitch Glossary*) using the pink and cream ribbons mentioned in *Materials* and stitch in place, embroidering reverse ribbon leaves and twisted ribbon leaves in no-green and gold-striped ribbons, alternating colours on each fuschia.

8   Using DMC pink and green, embroider three straight stitches in centre of each fuchsia with three pink buds on each stem.

9   Using no-green rayon ribbon embroider large lazy daisy leaves around design and embroider two straight stitches over the top with DMC Perle in pale green.

10   Using pink silver-edged ribbon embroider reverse ribbon stitch to form large buds as shown.

11   Make three ribbon leaves using lime green luminous ribbon and stitch in place.

12   Make cushion up with piping and sew tassels in place.

Lady Chantale-Therese

*I love to use these silk pictures in my work, when I can add braids and ribbons
to enhance the colours within the picture. Once you choose a silk picture
and match material, ribbons, braids and threads to the colours of
your picture, the result is beautiful.*

Materials

- craft glue
- 1 silk picture — 26 cm x 18 cm approximately
- 63 cm x 53 cm (56 cm x 46 cm when made up) champagne silk Jacquard
- 0.5 m Mokuba gold metallic braid 0863 col. 34
- 0.5 m Mokuba 80027 col. 3 (turquoise), 35 mm wide (for side panels)
- 0.5 m Mokuba grosgrain 9000 col. 44 (turquoise), 6 mm wide
- 1 m Mokuba 4522 col. 18 (turquoise), 40 mm (for bow)
- 0.5 m Mokuba 4881 col. 1, 25 mm wide (graduation organdy)
- 0.5 m Mokuba 4597 col. 14 (gold stripe), 8 mm wide
- 4 m Mokuba rayon ribbon 1505 col. 18 (grey/green), 12 mm wide
- 0.5 m gold wire-edged ribbon, 25 mm wide
- 2 m Mokuba 4647 (pleated) col. 15 (gold), 15 mm wide
- 0.5 m Mokuba 4570 col. 19 (metallic apricot), 15 mm wide
- 1 m Mokuba tubular organdy 4650 col. 19 (blue), 25 mm wide
- 3 m Mokuba tubular organdy 4650 col. 1 (gold), 25 mm wide
- 2m Mokuba organdy 4563 col. 1 (soft apricot), 25 mm wide
- 2 m Mokuba 4599 col. 9 (no-green), 13 mm wide (leaves)
- 1 m Mokuba rayon ribbon 1505 col. 15 (beige), 12 mm wide
- 3 m pure silk ribbon col. 74 (turquoise), 4 mm wide (lazy daisy leaves)
- DMC 928 (pale blue)
- 1 m Mokuba 4645 col. 45 (gold), 11 mm wide
- 1 m turquoise Thai silk for backing and ruche

Method

1   Using craft glue, dab small dots along edges of silk picture and position on the centre of material — allow ten minutes to dry. This makes the job of stitching the picture in place much easier.

2   Tack along edge of picture to completely secure.

3   Lay gold braid, wide turquoise ribbon, and narrow grosgrain ribbon along both sides of picture and stitch in place as shown in the photograph.

4   Using fancy-edged turquoise ribbon make a bow and stitch at top of work, gently pushing the ribbon to form soft pleats and stitching to hold each pleat.

5   Make a ribbon rose using graduation organdy to form a shaded rose.

6   Embroider reverse ribbon leaves in gold-striped ribbon and grey/green rayon ribbon around rose to complete top section of picture.

7   Make a bow using gold wire-edged ribbon and stitch at bottom centre of picture.

8   Make a large ribbon rose using graduation organdy to create a bicoloured rose.

9   Using the pleated gold ribbon, embroider two flannel flowers at either side of bow, as shown in the photograph and template.

10 Make two ribbon roses using the metallic apricot gold-edged ribbon and stitch either side of flannel flowers.

11 Using the organdy ribbon colours make nine ribbon roses and stitch seven of them in a line from under the left flannel flower continuing to the right flannel flower. Sew remaining two roses centrally under this line of roses as shown. Embroider reverse ribbon leaves around all these roses in alternating no-green rayon and grey/green ribbons.

12 Make sweet pea flowers from soft apricot and gold organdy ribbons and stitch in place, embroidering reverse ribbon leaves on either side (in Mokuba beige and no-green ribbons). These leaves may need to be secured in the centre to keep them flat and also to ensure the raw edge of flowers are covered.

13 Embroider remaining lazy daisy leaves in pure silk ribbon (turquoise).

14 Straight stitch stems on all sweet peas, in DMC 928 (pale blue) using two strands, taking these stems under the roses.

15 Make a double bow using gold satin ribbon and stitch among roses where shown.

16 Make up cushion using the turquoise silk for a 2 cm ruche and the backing of the cushion.

Above: template for Lady Chantale-Therese Cushion at 60%.

Black Victorian Collar

I was very fortunate to find this beautiful Victorian collar intact and with its original rosette at the neck. The rich creamy gold fabric is a stark contrast to the delicate black lace. I had a beautiful cameo reminiscent of the Victorian era in my collections and used it to compliment the collar. I added a velvet ribbon, gold braid, several jet beads and found a complimentary frame — the result is striking.

Materials

- black Victorian lace collar — antique shops
- 58 cm x 58 cm cream/gold fabric
- 1 m Mokuba velvet frilled ribbon 4585 col. 3 (black), 28 mm wide
- cameo decoration
- 28 cm braid Mokuba 0863 col. 34 (gold)
- 29 black jet beads
- 0.25 m black silk or satin ribbon 15 mm wide

Method

1   Gently stitch collar around edge and centre to secure to the fabric.

2   Make a bow using velvet frilled ribbon and stitch in place, curling at both ends as shown and stitching to hold.

3   Place cameo in centre of collar and stitch in place.

4   Attach gold braid around cameo and stitch jet beads in each hole of the braid.

5   Make a black rose and stitch in centre of bow.

6   Frame in a suitable old-fashioned frame to add to the period style of this piece.

Millinery Delight & Classical Carnation

Hat boxes today are not only used to store a beautiful hat, they are used to house a myriad of keepsakes. There are many decorative hat boxes already available but to create your own is truly a lovely way to store your most precious treasures.

If you don't feel comfortable making up the hat box yourself, do the embroidery and take it to a skilled seamstress, such as Elaine Lee, Le Collections, 116 Union Road, Surrey Hills 3127 (03 9888 4977) to make up the box.

As I have already mentioned, ribbons come in many colours, textures and patterns — often the ribbon itself can give you a hint on how it could be utilised in a floral design. This was the case with the ribbon used to make this Carnation Cushion, because its crinkling design immediately made me think of carnations — I think the results are quite delightful.

Millinery Delight — Materials

- 1 m upholstery damask or any other sturdy fabric
- 3 m double-sided satin ribbon (beige), 25 mm wide
- 2.5 m single-sided satin ribbon (cream), 25 mm wide
- 2 m Mokuba moire ribbon 1400 col. 12 (cream), 36 mm wide
- 3 m satin-edged Mokuba 4546 col. 12 (cream), 15 mm wide
- 3 m rayon Mokuba 1512 col. 12 (beige), 8 mm wide
- 4 m Mokuba 4597 col. 14 (gold stripe), 15 mm wide
- DMC Perle 644 (pale green)
- 8 m variegated chenille thread (pink/cream)
- DMC 3052 (green)
- white Madeira floss
- gold Glista thread
- cream Madeira floss

Method

1   Cut fabric 43 cm x 43 cm square — this will easily allow enough to cover a hat box lid up to 30 cm in diameter.

2   Make four large tea roses and one small, with ribbons in creams and beige as shown and stitch in a circle in centre of fabric face.

3   Make four large ribbon roses, again using the cream and beige ribbons, and stitch in place.

4   Using gold-striped ribbon embroider lazy daisy leaves and reverse ribbon leaves around cluster of roses.

5   Embroider large ribbon buds using cream satin-edged ribbon with reverse ribbon leaves and lazy daisy leaves where shown.

6   Attach buds with DMC Perle (pale green) in a straight stitch.

7 Using Mokuba beige ribbon and chenille thread embroider ribbon buds and straight stitch buds. Attach these to central roses with DMC 3052 (green), using one strand.

8 With white Madeira floss, embroider straight stitch buds in place with gold Glista bullion buds either side and using a straight stitch for stem.

9 Scatter lazy daisy leaves at base of stems in DMC Perle (pale green), and finish with French knots in cream Madeira floss scattered all around rose design.

Classical Carnation — Materials

- 3 m Mokuba 4647 col. 29 (dusky pink), 38 mm wide
- 3 m Mokuba 4647 col. 12 (cream), 38 mm wide
- 0.5 m Elizabeth silk Duchess satin col. Blush; cushion face measures 30 cm x 30 cm when made up
- 2 m Mokuba 4597 col. 14 (gold stripe organdy), 15 mm wide
- 2 m Mokuba 4599 col. 9 (no-green), 15 mm wide
- DMC Perle 644 (pale green)
- gold Madeira floss
- 0.5 m cream pleated material for frill

Method

1 Make up two dusky pink and three cream carnations and stitch to material face.

2 Make three dusky pink and three cream carnation buds and sew these in place also as shown on design.

3 Using Mokuba ribbon with gold stripe, work lazy daisy leaves around carnations where shown and embroider reverse ribbon leaves on carnation bud.

4 Using Mokuba no-green rayon ribbon, embroider remaining reverse ribbon leaves on buds.

5 Using DMC perle (pale green) embroider straight stitch stems on all buds and leaves where shown and embroider straight stitch leaves by first making a central long stitch and embroidering stitches shorter on either side until you achieve a leaf shape.

6 With gold floss embroider several straight stitches over lazy daisy ribbon leaves to create a sheen. I have also embroidered a couple of straight stitches over some of the larger leaves as well.

7 Make cushion up using pleated material as frill.

Sweet Pea Fairy Dreams

I was given a small bowl with this fairy for the lid and thought it would make an enchanting embroidery. As I have two boys, I have now become very popular with my god-daughters since creating these fairy pieces.

Although my boys are interested in watching as the embroidery takes shape neither boy has jumped at the opportunity of having Sweet Pea Fairy Dreams on their bedroom wall!

Materials

- 1 m Mokuba silk gorgette ribbon 4472 col. 40 (dusky apricot), 25 mm wide
- 1 m Mokuba silk gorgette ribbon 4472 col. 31 (soft apricot), 25 mm wide
- 1 m Mokuba silk gorgette ribbon 4472 col. 29 (soft plum), 25 mm wide
  (note that the above silk gorgette ribbons can be substituted with wide pure silk ribbons in colours as shown; remember to paint edgess in gold fabric paint as below.)
- gold fabric paint to paint on edge of flimsy ribbons
  craft or tacky glue
- fairy piece — available from fairy or gift shops
- 50 cm x 50 cm pale pink Thai silk
- 1.5 m Mokuba 4617 col. 7 (gold metallic organdy), 25 mm wide
- 3 m Mokuba 1500 col. 40 (dusky pink organdy), 25 mm wide
- 0.5 m Mokuba 4570 col. 18 (pink metallic gold edge), 15 mm wide
- 1 m Mokuba 4546 col. 29 (dusky pink satin edge), 15 mm wide
- 1 m Mokuba 4570 col. 1 (white silver metallic), 15 mm wide
- 1 m dusky pink single-sided satin ribbon, 8 mm wide
- 0.5 m apricot nylon ribbon, 8 mm wide
- 0.5 m Mokuba 4546 col. 31 (pale pink satin-edge ribbon), 15 mm wide
- 4 m pure silk ribbon col. 162 (pale pink), 7 mm wide
- cream Madeira floss
- 2 m Mokuba 4597 col. 14 (gold stripe), 8 mm wide
- DMC Perle 644 (pale green) — stems of pink flannel flowers
- 3 m Mokuba 1500 col. 31 (green organdy), 8 mm wide
- DMC 3012 (green) — 1 strand for stems of sweet pea
- 3 m Mokuba 4563 col. 1 (apricot organdy), 8 mm wide
- 4 m pure silk ribbon col. 135 (apricot), 4 mm wide
- DMC 644 (green) — 1 strand for bud stems
- 3 m Mokuba 1500 col. 18 (pink organdy), 8 mm wide
- glitter glue
- variety coloured glitters

Method

1. Paint the edges of silk gorgette ribbons with gold fabric paint and allow to dry (these are to be used for sweet peas).

2. Using craft or tacky glue, secure fairy piece in centre of fabric.

3. Starting with the largest rose and working around fairy, make a ribbon rose combining gold metallic ribbon and dusky pink organdy ribbon and secure at centre base of fairy.

4. Make up other ribbon roses in colours as shown in photograph and secure to material. The two roses at either side of the top of fairy are made by combining gold metallic and pale pink satin-edged ribbon.

5. Embroider flannel flowers using pure silk pale pink ribbon and working straight stitches for the centres in cream floss.

6. On either side of flannel flowers, embroider reverse ribbon leaves in gold stripe ribbon and embroider a long straight stitch in DMC Perle pale green as stem.

7. Make sweet peas in various shades of silk flimsy ribbon (using detailed instructions in *Techniques and Stitch Glossary*) and sew in place as shown, embroidering reverse ribbon leaves in green organdy ribbon. Stems are worked in green DMC 3012, one strand.

8. Using narrow apricot organdy ribbon and apricot pure silk ribbon, embroider hanging ribbon buds starting with organdy ribbon first and finishing with smaller more delicate buds in pure silk. Join stems on all buds using green DMC 644, one strand.

9. Using one strand green DMC 3012, embroider sweet pea curls in stem stitch where shown.

10. Embroider remaining buds in narrow apricot organdy with pale pink organdy either side as straight stitches.

11. Embroider reverse ribbon leaves in gold stripe and green organdy ribbon around and over fairy piece.

12. Finally, dab glitter glue over fairy and sprinkle with colourful glitter.

13. I have chosen an old frame I found in an antique shop. I took the mirror out, gilded over the damaged and worn metal and glued glitter on several flowers to achieve an original and beautiful picture. The whole effect was finished off by obtaining a convex piece of Perspex to protect the embroidery.

Above: template for Sweet Pea Fairy Dreams at 75% (instructions begin on page 25).

Crystal Iceberg

Being a bower-bird at heart I have collected a wide assortment of treasures over the years and I'm always thrilled when I can find a special place to put some of them. In my large nest of collections I had an assortment of old crystal and glass buttons just waiting to make up a large crystal vase.

Materials

- 67 cm x 71 cm pale blue damask
- 1 m Mokuba 4546 col. 00 (white), 15 mm wide
- 2 m white nylon ribbon, 25 mm wide
- 4 m white one-sided satin ribbon, 15 mm wide
- 4 m white pure silk ribbon, 10 mm wide
- 1 m pale green satin ribbon, 25 mm wide
- 4 m Mokuba 4597 col. 14 (gold stripe organdy), 15 mm wide
- large assortment of old crystal and glass buttons (I have used 51 all together)
- 10 extra crystal buttons (to decorate frame)
- 16 blue crystal beads (to decorate frame)

Flower combinations:

Wisteria
- 5 m pure silk ribbon col. 58 (grey), 7 mm wide
- DMC 775 (pale blue)
- 4 m pure silk ribbon col. 90 (pale blue), 4 mm wide
- DMC 762 (grey)
- DMC ecru
- DMC 524 (grey/green)

Chrysanthemums — Grey flowers
- 4 m pure silk ribbon col. 58 (grey), 4 mm wide
- DMC 524 (grey/green)
- white Madeira floss

Bluebells— Bells of Holland
- 3 m pure silk ribbon col. 74 (blue), 4 mm wide
- DMC 524 (grey/green)
- white Madeira floss

Queen Anne Lace
- DMC white
- DMC 524 (grey/green)

Camellia Star-above-Star — White flower
- 4 m white pure silk ribbon, 7 mm wide
- DMC 524 (grey/green)
- white Madeira floss

White Buds
- 7 m white pure silk ribbon, 4 mm wide
- DMC 524 (grey/green)

Method

1   Lightly draw outline of vase shape on to material (but stitch buttons on last of all as they are very heavy).

2   Make up ribbon roses in assorted white ribbons and secure them in position.

3   Make three pale green satin leaves using leaf stitch and secure them where shown.

4   Each wisteria is made up of four large grey silk ribbon buds (using colour 58) and straight stitch buds in DMC pale blue (three strands) on either side of the grey buds.

5   Under the four large grey buds, create four small pale blue silk ribbon buds (using colour 90). Straight stitch buds either side of pale blue buds using DMC grey (three strands). Embroider two DMC grey straight stitch buds, adding two DMC pale blue straight stitch buds at either side to complete bud groupings. You have now worked eight buds in total to form central core of wisteria.

6   Bullion stitches are placed at either side of buds in alternating colours of DMC pale blue and ecru, while DMC grey/green (one strand) is used for stems and also as lazy daisy leaves on all buds to join wisteria to ribbon rose mass.

7   Embroider remaining flowers in place following instructions contained in *Techniques and Stitch Glossary*, and using the colour combinations shown within *Materials* above.

8   Finally sew crystal and glass buttons in place to form shape of vase.

9   When your embroidery is framed, glue remaining buttons and beads onto the frame to highlight your design. I have also hand-painted some delicate flowers on the frame, but this is optional and depends on the type of frame you have chosen. I had two plain wooden frames joined together and then added interest with paint and crystals but there are many ornate frames available to suit this detailed embroidery.

Above: template for Crystal Iceberg vase at 50%.

Lily Pad, Silver Anniversary, Summertime Gerbera

Lily Pad is a whimsical cushion which shows how to carry a flower theme right through to the making of the actual cushion. With a simple, circular face, instead of adding a ruche or frill, you can make individual petals and sew each to the circle to create a delightful flower-shaped cushion.

In the 1800s, jewelled embroidery was very popular. While those examples were all done by hand, today we can buy superb embellished fabrics created in the manner of this past era. Although I enjoy doing hand-beading and bullion work, when I came across the bullion panel I have used in Silver Anniversary, I was delighted.

Finally, this cheeky gerbera cushion is a reminder of a bunch of gerberas given to me by a friend. To me they always create a sense of cheerfulness with their perky faces and I tried to capture one in embroidery.

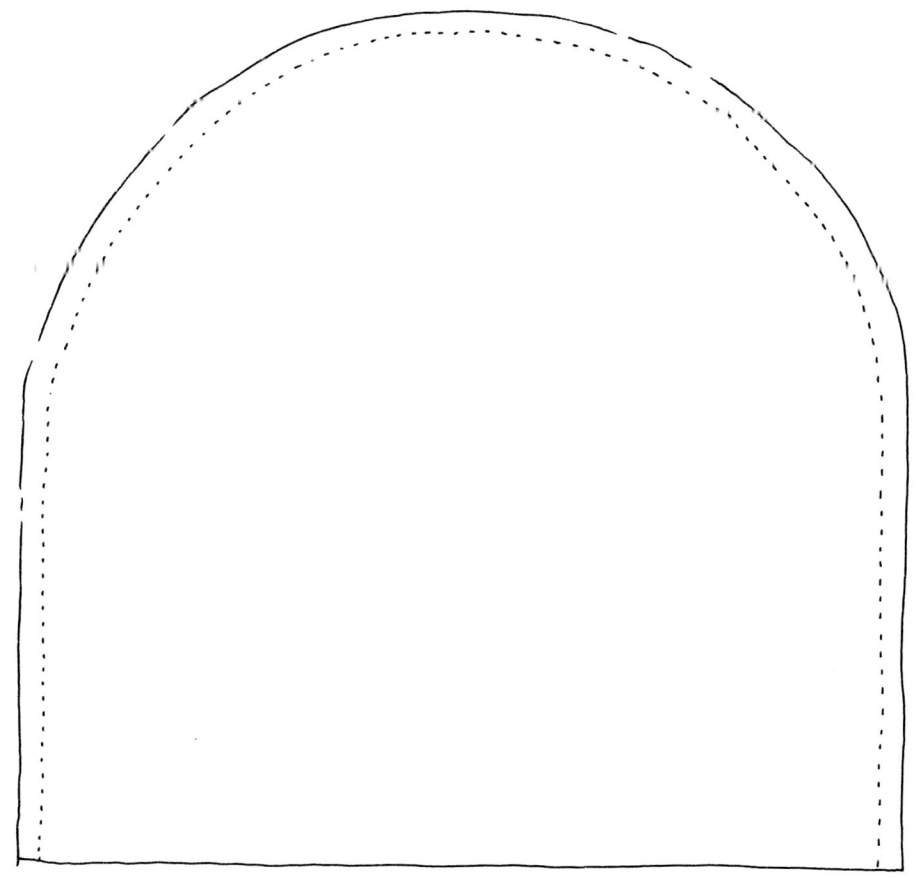

Above: Large Lily template for cushion at 100%.

Lily Pad — Materials

- 1 m Elizabeth silk Duchess satin, col. blush (from quality fabric stores such as Lincraft: bridal section). I used the cream side of fabric for face and the pink side for the piping covering and petal edging. In this project I used pale pink Thai silk for the petals, but would recommend using the reverse of the Duchess silk; add to above material allowance if you choose to do this.
- 2 m cream rayon ribbon, 15 mm wide
- 3 m Mokuba 1505 col. 15 (beige), 15 mm wide
- 3 m pure silk ribbon col. 162 (pale pink), 7 mm wide
- 3 m Mokuba 1540 col. 002 (pale pink), 7 mm wide
- Silf Butterfly Metallic Thread col. 402 (pink metallic)
- DMC ecru 644
- piping cord for edge of cushion face
- 0.5 m flat wadding to pad cushion

Method

1 Cushion face measures 28 cm x 28 cm when made up; I used a dinner plate to achieve the desired shape. (Use the larger petal template on previous page for the cushion lily petals.)

2 Make five small lilies using the lily petal template found in *Techniques and Stitch Glossary*, and sew at top of fabric face.

3 Make four cream ribbon roses and sew in place.

4 Using Mokuba beige rayon ribbon, embroider lazy daisy leaves around top of small lily and roses.

5 To make fuchsias use pale pink pure silk ribbon. Fuchsias are made by combining three reverse ribbon stitches in Mokuba pale pink and two reverse ribbon stitches in Mokuba beige ribbon as shown in *Techniques and Stitch Glossary*.

6 Stamens are embroidered straight stitches with one strand of Silf Metallic Thread. Add French knots in two strands of DMC ecru to end of stamens.

7 Embroider straight stitches in DMC ecru (two strands) coming down from each fuchsia — to give the effect of the fuchsia hanging.

8 Make up cushion face by first covering piping cord using the pink side of the silk, then adding the piping around cushion face. Make back of cushion the same way but this time use the cream side of the silk.

9 Make sixteen petals (from reverse pink side of Duchess silk or pink Thai silk) using the large petal template found on page 33 and stitch to face on wrong side.

10 Cut four circles from wadding slightly smaller than face and sew to back circle of cushion. Hand sew back of cushion to wrong side of face taking care not to show stitches on front of cushion.

11 Gently sculpt petals into curves. Add a small frog, fairy, cherub or dragonfly to small lily for a touch of whimsy and lily pad is complete.

Silver Anniversary — Materials

- 0.5 m silk silver bullion embroidered panel (from quality fabric stores such as Lincraft: bridal section)
- 0.75 m Elizabeth silk Duchess satin col. blush — (33 cm x 31 cm when made up) with 2 cm ruche
- 3 m Mokuba 1505 col. 5 (grey rayon), 12 mm wide
- cream Madeira floss
- 5 m Mokuba 1500 col. 23 (blue organdy), 11 mm wide
- 3 m pure silk ribbon col. 162 (pink), 7 mm wide
- silver bullion thread
- silver Glista thread
- 1 m silver cord

Method

1. Secure silver embroidered panel along centre of Duchess satin fabric.

2. Using Mokuba grey rayon ribbon, embroider three half flannel flowers along each side of the panel using cream floss in straight stitches to fill centres, and blue organdy ribbon to make two reverse ribbon leaves at base.

3. Embroider pink silk ribbon buds as shown with blue organdy reverse ribbon leaves either side coming from flannel flowers.

4. Embroider bullions in shape of leaves as shown, alternating silver threads.

5. Scatter lazy daisy leaves around flannel flowers in one strand silver Glista thread.

6. Embroider silver Glista fly stitches around pink buds and long straight stitches over blue leaves where shown.

7. Make up cushion with tight ruche and stitch silver cord bows into each corner.

Above: template for Silver Anniversary Cushion at 55%.

Summertime Gerbera — Materials

- 1 m Elizabeth silk Duchess satin col. blush
- 5 m pure silk ribbon col. 162 (pale pink), 7 mm wide
- DMC stranded cotton 907 (bright green)
- DMC stranded cotton 3341 (coral)
- DMC flower thread 2223 (pink)
- DMC stranded cotton 444 (bright yellow)
- 2 m Mokuba 1513 col. 31 (pale pink)
- 2 m pure silk ribbon col. 56 (lime green), 4 mm wide
- DMC Perle 644 (pale green)
- 1 m pink cord

Method

1. Duchess satin is a beautiful fabric to work with. I have used the cream side for the cushion face and I suggest using the blush side for the frill or choose a pink Thai silk for the frill. Material face measures 35 cm x 25 cm when made up and frill measure 7 cm. (I used a serving plate to achieve oval shape.)

2. The gerberas are made by using 7 mm pure silk in pale pink and working long reverse ribbon stitches around a circle — making some stitches slightly longer than others.

3. Then embroider French knots using DMC bright green (three strands) in a smaller central circle.

4. Around this central circle embroider French knots in DMC coral (three strands).

5. Using DMC pink flower thread, embroider straight stitches all around the central circle to outer edge and then continue French knots around outer edge in DMC coral (three strands).

6. With DMC bright yellow, using one strand, embroider straight stitches randomly over flower thread stitches to give depth to the gerbera centre.

7. Then using one strand of DMC coral, work straight stitches out along some petals of the gerbera.

8. To embroider the half open gerbera use a combination of pale pink silk ribbon and Mokuba pale pink cotton ribbon as shown and with the lime green pure silk ribbon embroider reverse ribbon leaves to form base of flower.

9. With lime green pure silk ribbon gently stitch down centre of ribbon length approximately 16 cm and 21 cm on both flowers to attach stem and then embroider stem stitch in DMC Perle pale green down centre of each stem.

10. Make up cushion with 7 cm frill and sew on pink cord to finish.

Spring Garden

Definitely not for feet!

Materials

- 72 cm x 57cm mauve moire tafetta (measures 48 cm x 37 cm when made up)
- footstool
- DMC 3041 (grape) (4 strands — satin stitch ribbon and bows)

Dark Purple Grapes:
- DMC 208 (dark purple) — 3 strands — French knots
- DMC 470 (green) — 2 strands — lazy daisy leaves and stem

Light Purple Grapes:
- DMC 340 (light purple) — 3 strands — French knots
- DMC 470 (green) — 2 strands — lazy daisy leaves and stem

Half Daisy:
- DMC 210 (lilac) — 3 strands — lazy daisy petals filled in with three straight stitches
- DMC Ecru — 2 strands — three French knots
- DMC 647 (green) — 2 strands — lazy daisy leaves and stem

Star Flower:
- DMC 211 (pale lilac) — 2 strands — straight stitches
- DMC 3047 (dusky lemon) — 2 strands — French knots — one wrap
- DMC 470 (green) — 2 strands — lazy daisy leaves filled in with three straight stitches

Iris:
- DMC 552 (deep purple) — 2 strands — two small split buds
- DMC 745 (lemon) — 1 strand — two straight stitches in centre of Iris
- DMC 581 (green) — 2 strands — fly stitch and long lazy daisy leaves

Bullions:
- DMC 315 (plum) — 2 strands — 30 wraps around needle
- DMC 208 (medium purple) — 2 strands — straight stitch buds either side
- DMC 520 (dark green) — 2 strands — lazy daisy leaves, straight stitch stem

Light Mauve buds:
- DMC 3743 (light mauve) — 3 strands — straight stitch buds
- DMC 523 (green) — 1 strand — fly stitch, lazy daisy leaves

Pink buds:
- DMC 3727 (dusky pink) ⎫
- DMC 3608 (bright pink) ⎬ 3 strands — straight stitch buds
- DMC 224 (pink) ⎭
- DMC 523 (green) — 1 strand fly stitch and stem

Deep Purple Lazy Daisy:
- DMC 550 (deep purple) — 2 strands
- DMC Ecru — 2 strands French knots
- DMC 600 (hot pink) — 3 strands — scattered French knots throughout design
- DMC 912 (green) — 1 strand — lazy daisy leaves scattered throughout design
- 1 m mauve braid for detail around footstool

Method

1   Embroider satin stitch ribbon and bows in centre of fabric using DMC grape-coloured thread.

2   Embroider stitches randomly among satin stitch bows using colours and stitches as detailed in *Materials*, and following photograph and template.

3   Have footstool covered by a reputable upholsterer.

Above: template for Spring Garden footstool at 66%.

Chatelaine

Over the years I have collected some interesting antique sewing implements, and I am always adding to my collection. I thought it might be nice to incorporate some of these precious items in an embroidery and make a lasting heirloom.

The pieces I have used include a beautiful enamel scissor holder which would have been originally attached to a chatelaine. Chatelaines were worn by Victorian ladies, especially in France, on a belt around their waist whilst they embroidered so they had all the necessary equipment easily and practically to hand.

I have also incorporated a beautifully decorated needlecase — 'The Louise' — (dating from around 1870) that, when opened, has several beautifully carved and numbered compartments. Other items include an intricate silver gilt crochet hook (dating from around 1830), mother-of-pearl items: silk winder (about 1800), stiletto (about 1820) and reel holder (about 1840), carved wooden acorn used to hold needles and thimble, lace-making bobbins, velvet strawberry pincushion from around 1860, a bodkin used for tapestry and ribbon work, and, of course, a thimble.

Materials

- central antique piece
- tacky craft glue
- 50 cm x 50 cm gold silk satin
- 0.5 m Mokuba 4546 col. 26 (dark purple), 15 mm wide for fuchsias
- 0.5 m Mokuba 4546 col. 92 (purple), 15 mm wide for fuchsias
- gold Madeira floss (straight stitch buds on stamens)
- Anchor 281 (green) (stamens on fuchsias — 1 strand)
- 1.5 m Mokuba 4597 col. 14 (gold-striped organdy), 8 mm wide (for all ribbon leaves on fuchsias)
- 2 m Mokuba 1540 col. 156 (lilac), 7 mm wide (for purple flannel flowers with gold floss centres)
- 2 m Mokuba 4563 col. 5 (turquoise organdy), 8 mm wide (for all ribbon leaves on flannel flowers)
- 1 m Mokuba 1505 col. 27 (lilac), 15 mm wide (small ribbon roses)
- 1 m Mokuba 4563 col. 11 (blue), 15 mm wide (small ribbon roses)
- 1 m Mokuba 4599 col. 14 (plum), 5 mm wide (ribbon buds)
- DMC 552 (mauve) (straight stitch buds either side of Mokuba ribbon buds — 3 strands)
- DMC 368 (green) (used for stems and lazy daisy leaves — 1 strand)
- 2 m lime green pure silk ribbon, 4 mm wide
- DMC 210 (lilac) (grapes — 3 strands, 2 wraps)
- 2 m pure silk ribbon col. 117 (vibrant blue), 4 mm wide (silk ribbon buds)
- DMC 327 (purple) (grub buds — 2 strands, 25 wraps)
- 0.25 m rose Thai silk
- 1 m Mokuba 4560 col. 15 (gold organdy print ribbon), 25 mm wide
- 1 m Mokuba 4561 col. 15 (gold organdy print ribbon), 25 mm wide

Method

1   Glue antique piece in centre of material with tacky craft glue.

2   Embroider six fuschias (three in Mokuba dark purple and three in Mokuba purple ribbons) using gold floss and green Anchor thread for stamens. Embroider reverse ribbon leaves either side of the fuschias in gold striped ribbon.

3   Embroider five flannel flowers in lilac ribbon with gold floss French knot centres and turquoise organdy ribbon leaves.

4   Make five ribbon roses combining Mokuba lilac and blue ribbons together and stitch into place as shown.

5   Embroider large ribbon buds in Mokuba plum ribbon using DMC mauve three strands to form a straight stitch bud either side of each ribbon bud. Using two strands DMC green embroider two straight stitches over plum ribbon buds and stem. On alternate buds embroider small reverse ribbon leaves as shown using lime green pure silk ribbon.

6   Embroider French knots using DMC lilac where shown.

7   Using vibrant blue pure silk ribbon, embroider ribbon buds and trailing from these use DMC purple for long bullion bud. Embroider all stems in DMC green.

8   Scatter small lazy daisy leaves around edge of work using DMC greens in one strand.

9   Have your framer mount picture using rose Thai silk to cover mount. Use Mokuba organdy ribbons to create a border around this mount as shown in the photograph and attach antique pieces to picture with craft glue. Have framed in suitable frame.

Above: template of Chatelaine at 72%.

Sumptuous Straw

Gone are the days when embroidery was restricted to doilies and tablecloths. This bag really represents new age embroidery at its boldest. The luscious floppy roses combined with the basic straw bag really create a bit of fun, and this roomy hold-all becomes a colourful showpiece.

Materials

- 1.5 m Mokuba 0496 col. 36 (turquoise), 75 mm wide (pleated organdy)
- large straw bag
- 5 m Mokuba 4546 col. 29 (dusky pink satin-edged), 50 mm wide
- 2 m Mokuba 4650 col. 18 (lilac), 50 mm wide (tubular organdy)
- 4 m Mokuba 4617 col. 2 (turquoise), 25 mm wide (metallic organdy for large buds)
- 3 m Mokuba 4599 col. 5 (lime green), 15 mm wide
- 2 m Mokuba 4650 col. 22 (green organdy), 25 mm wide
- 2 m Mokuba 4563 col. 5 (turquoise), 15 mm wide (reverse ribbon leaves on metallic organdy buds)
- 2 m Mokuba 1505 col. 27 (lilac), 15 mm wide (hanging lilac buds)
- 0.5 m Mokuba 4595 col. 9 (luminous turquoise), 25 mm wide (ribbon buds)
- 1.5 m lilac wire-edged ribbon, 25 mm wide (made in Switzerland)
- 1.5 m lilac shot-with-green wire-edged ribbon, 25 mm wide (made in Switzerland)
- 1 m Mokuba 4563 col. 6 (pale blue organdy), 8 mm wide
- DMC stranded 733 (lime green)

Method

1 Stitch turquoise pleated organdy ribbon along top of bag.

2 Make a large frilled rose using dusky pink satin-edged ribbon and stitch in centre of the pleated ribbon.

3 Make two large ribbon roses combining the dusky pink satin-edged ribbon and lilac tubular organdy ribbon. Sew extra satin-edged ribbon around the edge of both of these roses to create frilled roses, and stitch in place either side of centre rose. Make two more large ribbon roses combining satin-edged dusky pink and lilac organdy ribbons as above, but without frilled effect, and sew these into place, using the photograph as a guide. Make two extra ribbon roses combining turquoise metallic organdy and dusky pink satin-edged ribbons and stitch beneath centre rose.

4 Embroider large lazy daisy leaves in lime green ribbon around large roses as shown.

5 Using the wide green organdy ribbon, embroider large reverse ribbon leaves around large roses.

6 Make six sweet pea flowers and attach to bag using appropriate green ribbons in reverse ribbon stitch either side — securing each leaf with a stitch to hold in place.

7 With metallic organdy and lilac ribbons embroider ribbon buds where shown and use the thin green organdy ribbon for leaves either side where appropriate.

8 To finish, use narrow pale blue organdy ribbon and embroider small ribbon buds hanging from lilac buds and attach with fly ribbon buds hanging from stitch stems in DMC 733 (lime green) two strands.

Pearl Drops, Queen Anne Bolster, Fleur de Lys

These cushions and the bolster are simple examples of the wonderful fabrics you can buy that you can quickly make into elaborate-looking accessories. I found all these lovely materials in Lincraft's bridal section, but quality fabric stores everywhere will be able to help you with a selection of sumptuous fabrics.

The Pearl Drops cushion is perfect to compliment a heavily adorned embroidered piece, while the Queen Anne bolster is made using a superb gold embroidered material with only a little ribbon detail.

The Fleur de Lys cushion shows the interesting effect achieved when you reverse material and create a contrast in colour. With this particular fabric I couldn't decide which side to use, so I used both. If you do use a patterned material like this Fleur de Lys design, one crucial factor is to match the pattern as shown here — it gives a far more professional result.

Pearl Drops — Materials

- 0.5 m silk metallic embroidered net with pearl and bullion detail
  — cushion measures 38 cm x 38 cm made up
- 0.5 m cream Duchess satin (for cushion backing)
- piping which is covered in Duchess satin
- 1 tassel

Method

1 Make up cushion using the Duchess satin as backing.
2 Add piping and then add gold tassel to the centre of cushion.

Queen Anne Bolster — Materials

- 1 m cream silk with gold embroidery
- bolster insert
- 5 m Mokuba 4546 col. 12 (cream), 15 mm wide (for flannel flowers and ribbon roses)
- 3 m Mokuba 1500 col. 15 (beige organdy), 8 mm wide
- 2 m Mokuba 4599 col. 9 (no-green rayon), 15 mm wide
- 1 m Mokuba 4597 col. 14 (gold stripe organdy), 15 mm wide
- 9 pearl drops
- 2 cream tassels
- 2 gold flowerettes

Method

1   Measure fabric over bolster insert and cut to appropriate length.

2   Embroider nine flannel flowers with Mokuba cream ribbon, contrasting reverse ribbon leaf detail using beige organdy and no-green rayon ribbons.

3   Make four ribbon roses using cream ribbon and stitch where shown, embroidering reverse ribbon leaves in gold stripe and beige organdy ribbons.

4   Sew pearl drops in centre of flannel flowers.

5   Make up bolster cover and attach tassels and flowerettes to each end.

Fleur de Lys — Materials

- 0.5 m silk Herald Collection Fleur de Lys, colour blush
- 0.5 m Elizabeth silk Duchess satin, colour blush (for back of cushion, piping and ruche)
- 1.5 m Mokuba 4000 col. 65 (pink) narrow velvet cord (cut in three equal lengths and plaited)
- 0.25 m Mokuba 9307 col. 12 (cream) rosebud braid
- 1 m Mokuba 1505 col. 15 (beige), 15 mm wide
- 2 m Mokuba 4546 col. 29 (dusky pink), 15 mm wide
- 1 m Mokuba 4570 col. 4 (white silver-edged), 15 mm wide
- 1 m Mokuba 4599 col. 9 (no-green), 15 mm wide
- 1 m Mokuba 1505 col. 10 (silver), 15 mm wide
- DMC 734 (green)
- 2 m pure silk ribbon col. 56 (lime green), 4 mm wide
- 0.5 m Mokuba 4647 col. 29 (dusky pink crinkled ribbon), 38 mm wide
- cute cherub
- tacky glue

Method

1   Cut centre panel 34 cm x 34 cm square (measures 31 cm x 31 cm when sewn down) and pipe using Duchess satin.

2   Plait equal lengths of narrow velvet cord and sew in a circle 14 cms diameter.

3   Cut the green leaves from the rosebud braid and stitch the braid in place inside velvet cord circlet.

4   Make three ribbon roses using beige rayon ribbon; two ribbon roses combining dusky pink satin-edged and beige rayon ribbon; two ribbon roses combining dusky pink satin-edged and white silver-edged metallic ribbon and stitch in place in between cream rose-bud braid roses.

5   Embroider lazy daisy leaves in no-green rayon ribbon where shown and embroider ribbon buds using silver rayon ribbon.

6   With one strand of DMC green, embroider straight stitch stems on buds and lazy daisy leaves scattered around all ribbon roses.

7   Embroider lazy daisy leaves on either side of cream rosebuds using lime green pure silk ribbon.

8   Make up crinkled bow with dusky pink crinkled ribbon and stitch in place.

9   Glue cupid in position using tacky glue.

10 Stitch central panel to other side of remaining material, making sure you match the pattern, and make up cushion (measures 43 cm x 43 cm without ruche) with a 2 cm ruche in Duchess satin.

Fairy Pavlova

Making this fairy costume reminded me of my childhood years as a budding ballerina and our one big concert at the Princess theatre. I was only very young and in awe of the principal ballerinas in their billowing costumes and glittering tutus.

Materials

- 0.5 m pale pink tulle
- 0.5 m fine lilac tulle
- 0.5 m mauve tulle
- 0.5 m fine pink tulle
- 0.5 m elastic, 5 mm wide
- 9 m Mokuba 4546 col. 31 (pink), 25 mm wide (bows)
- 3 m Mokuba 4617 col. 2 (metallic blue), 25 mm wide (smaller bows)
- 2 m white silver-edged ribbon, 25 mm wide (bows)
- 2 m Mokuba 4650 col. 18 (lilac), 25 mm wide (tubular organdy)
- glitter glue
- glitter
- 20 crystals

Method

1   Cut scallops along edge of pale pink, fine lilac and mauve tulle — do not cut fine pink tulle at this stage.

2   Gather the heavier fine pink tulle along top edge with a long running stitch to fit length of elastic waistband. You can do this on a machine using elasticised thread or you can hand sew as I do.

3   Repeat this gathering process with other scallop-edged tulle layers finishing with a lilac layer.

4   Using fine pink tulle, cut a length of material 30 cm deep, fold in half and stitch together to make a wide strip. Gather this around outside edge of band and pull up at equal lengths around costume to form a scallop effect.

5   Make five pink bows 1.5 metres long and stitch in place, sewing one on either side of back opening very securely. (I have used one length from each side to tie dress together.)

6   Make five smaller metallic blue bows and three white silver-edged ribbon bows and stitch on top of pink bows.

7   Make five ribbon roses by combining pink and lilac organdy ribbons and stich in place.

8   Squeeze glitter glue around scallops on bottom layer of tulle and sprinkle glitter. Allow to dry.

9   Hand stitch crystals randomly over outside layer. Now you have a beautiful fairy dress for a budding ballerina!

Fairy Halo

Materials

- 0.5 m wire size 2 mm (from hardware store)
- 6 m Mokuba 4546 col. 31 (pink), 25 mm wide
- 0.5 m Mokuba 4617 col. 2 (blue metallic organdy), 25 mm wide
- 1 m white silver-edged ribbon, 25 mm wide
- 2 m Mokuba 4650 col. 18 (lilac tubular organdy), 50 mm wide
- 6 m Mokuba 1500 col. 23 (blue organdy), 5 mm wide
- several small pieces of pink tulle from fairy dress
- 6 crystal beads

Method

1   Measure your fairy's head and shape wire to fit.

2   Wrap Mokuba pink ribbon around wire and stitch at join.

3   Make ten pink ribbon roses and stitch evenly around halo.

4   Using blue metallic organdy ribbon, wide white silver-edged ribbon and lilac tubular ribbon, make three loops from each ribbon by folding 20 cm lengths in half and stitching alternate colours in between each ribbon rose.

5   Make several loops using narrow (5 mm) blue organdy ribbon and stitch these in between each rose, over the top of ribbons which are already in place.

6   Sew small pieces of tulle randomly behind several roses.

7   Sew crystal beads (three together) in the front of the halo in between three roses only.

8   Fairy wings: I shaped wire to wing shapes, covered them with white stockings and sprinkled glitter along glue lines, but you can easily buy fairy wings and attach them with Velcro.

Sweet Pea Posy

When I was young, I loved to play in my grandmother's garden. As soon as I arrived at her house, I would rush outside and spend what seemed to be hours among her flowers. She was English and had such an assortment of old-fashioned roses, hydrangeas, a heavenly lavender hedge and much, much more. But my absolute favourite by far was the sweet pea. I remember them being so much taller than me and smelling so sweet. These sweet pea remind me of her.

Materials

- gold fabric paint to paint edges of silk gorgette ribbon
- 2 m Mokuba silk gorgette ribbon 4472 col. 31 (soft apricot), 25 mm wide
- 2 m Mokuba silk gorgette ribbon 4472 col. 40 (dusky apricot), 25 mm wide
- 2 m Mokuba silk gorgette ribbon 4472 col. 29 (plum), 25 mm wide
- 2 m Mokuba silk gorgette ribbon 4472 col. 12 (cream), 25 mm wide
  (note that the above silk gorgette ribbons can be substituted with wide pure silk ribbons in colours as shown, remember to paint edges in gold fabric paint)
- 57 cm x 61 cm cream Duchess satin (Lincraft stores)
- 2 m Mokuba 4599 ribbon col. 9 (no-green rayon), 15 mm wide
- 5 m pure silk ribbon col. 56 (lime green), 4 mm wide
- DMC 3013 (green) — 2 strands for stems
- 0.75 m Mokuba 4560 ribbon col. 15 (gold organdy with gold fancy pattern), 40 mm wide

Method

1 Paint the edges of the silk gorgette ribbon with gold fabric paint and allow to dry.

2 Make sweet pea flowers in assorted colours of gorgette ribbon, using detailed instructions in *Techniques and Stitch Glossary*, and stitch in place.

3 Using no-green rayon ribbon and lime green pure silk ribbon, embroider reverse ribbon leaves on either side of sweet peas as shown.

4 Embroider stems and curls in stem stitch (see stitch glossary) using 2 strands DMC 3013 (green).

5 Make a bow using gold organdy ribbon and stitch in place.

6 Choose a frame to compliment your work.

Lilac Bordeaux, Buttercup Ivy, Formal Glory

These three designs use the simplicity of stencil patterns to create an interesting effect.

For Lilac Bordeaux I chose lilac fabric, used deep purple and mauve ribbons to highlight the grape stencil and I think the addition of velvet bobbles and braid around the edge of the cushion itself adds to the grape theme.

The Buttercup Ivy cushion shows just how effective the combination of stencils and embroidery can be. In just a few minutes with some simple brush strokes you can easily tranform a plain piece of fabric into a lavishly-designed piece before even beginning to learn to embroider. Add a few simple ribbon roses and buds and your design is complete.

The particular stencil I have chosen for the Formal Glory bolster has quite a formal pattern and lends itself for use, as I have shown, around each end of the bolster. It could also be used as a border on a square or rectangular cushion.

Lilac Bordeaux — Materials

- 45 cm x 45 cm (40 cm x 40 cm when made up) lilac moire taffeta (double the fabric requirements to create the back of cushion in the same fabric)
- grape stencil, stencil brush, green and gold fabric paint
- 1 m Mokuba ribbon 4546, col. 92 (purple), 15 mm wide (tea roses)
- 1 m lilac wire-edged ribbon, 25 mm wide, (ribbon roses)
- 0.5 m Mokuba ribbon 4595, col. 5 (purple luminous), 25 mm wide
- 7 silk leaves (available from quality fabric/craft stores, such as Lincraft)
- 7 velvet bobbles (Those in photographed project were bought in America but they can be substituted with bobbles taken from the braid mentioned below.)
- DMC 3746 (purple), 315 (burgundy)
- DMC 3011 (green)
- 3 m pure silk ribbon, col. 144 (pink), 4 mm wide
- 2 m pure silk ribbon, col. 56 (lime green), 4 mm wide
- 1 m Mokuba ribbon 4597, col. 14 (gold-striped organdy), 15 mm wide
- 0.5 m Mokuba ribbon 4546, col. 17 (green), 15 mm wide
- 1.5 m green and gold bobble braid
- 4 tassels with cord attached

Method

1   Stencil design on to fabric using green and gold fabric paint and alternating the colour of the grapes.

2   Allow to dry and iron on reverse side of fabric to set the paint.

3   Make up one tea rose using Mokuba purple ribbon and two ribbon roses using lilac wire-edged ribbon and sew above stencils as shown.

4   Using Mokuba 4595 (purple luminous) make three leaves using leaf stitch and attach in between each rose.

5   Sew silk or material leaves in place, at the same time adding the bobbles.

6   Using DMC 3746 (purple) and 315 (burgundy) — three strands of each — embroider bullions in position, alternating colours over worked piece. Take one strand of DMC 3011 (green) from each bullion as a long straight stitch back to the central rose to achieve the effect of hanging buds.

7   Scatter lazy daisy leaves created in DMC 3011 (green) as shown.

8   Work silk ribbon buds in col. 144 (pink) with reverse ribbon leaves either side in col. 56 (lime green) and stems in DMC 3011 (green).

9   Using gold-striped organdy and green Mokuba ribbons embroider reverse ribbon leaves around design as shown.

10 Make up cushion attaching bobble braid and tassels in each corner. Finish off by making a bow from tassel cord and securing it to each corner.

Buttercup Ivy — Materials

- 0.5 m buttercup yellow Thai silk or gold silk satin (57 cm x 42 cm when made up)
- ivy stencil, stencil brush, green fabric paint
- 0.5 m lilac wire-edged ribbon, 25 mm wide
- 1 m lilac shot-with-green wire-edged ribbon, 25 mm wide
- 0.5 m Mokuba 4546 col. 92 (purple), 15 mm wide
- 0.5 m Mokuba 4599 col. 14 (burgundy), 15 mm wide
- 0.5 m Mokuba 4546 col. 17 (dark green), 15 mm wide
- 0.5 m Mokuba 4480 col. 16 (lime green velvet), 25 mm wide
- 2 m Mokuba 1505 col. 27 (lilac), 15 mm wide
- 2 m pure silk ribbon col. 56 (lime green), 4 mm wide
- 3 m pure silk ribbon col. 163 (pink), 4 mm wide
- DMC 554 (lilac)
- DMC 340 (mauve)
- DMC 469 (green)
- DMC Perle 316 (dusky pink), 315 (plum)
- 4 m pure silk ribbon col. 84 (purple), 4 mm wide
- 1 m Mokuba 4597 col. 14 (gold stripe organdy), 15 mm wide
- 2 m piping cord
- 4 gold tassels

Method

1   Stencil ivy design onto fabric and when dry, iron on reverse side to set the paint.

2   Make one ribbon rose from lilac wire-edged ribbon, two roses from lilac shot-with-green wire-edged ribbon, two smaller roses with Mokuba purple, one small rose with Mokuba burgundy rayon and stitch all of them in place on centre of cushion in the middle of the stencilled ivy leaves.

3   Embroider reverse ribbon leaves around roses in Mokuba dark green ribbon. Make up three leaves using leaf stitch with Mokuba lime green velvet and stitch under roses as shown in the template and photograph.

4   Using Mokuba lilac ribbon, embroider three groups of large ribbon buds with reverse ribbon leaves either side of buds in pure silk lime green ribbon.

5   With pink pure silk ribbon embroider silk ribbon buds to each group of lilac buds and then using DMC lilac and mauve (three strands of each) alternate colours as shown and embroider bullion buds on each cluster.

6   To complete each group use one strand of DMC 469 (green) and embroider straight stitches from each bullion and bud to form stems and scatter lazy daisy leaves around clusters. I have left a couple of bullions in each group with no stem to add interest.

7   Using DMC perle 316 (dusky pink) and 315 (plum) embroider straight stitch buds to form grape effect with two lazy daisy leaves in pure silk lime green at the top of each grape.

8   To finish design, embroider silk ribbon buds in pure silk purple ribbon working buds over and over to make them quite chubby and using Mokuba gold stripe organdy ribbon as leaves over each bud.

9   Make up cushion with piping (covered in buttercup yellow silk) and attach four gold tassels to complete.

Above: template for Buttercup Ivy cushion at 50%.

57

Formal Glory — Materials

- 0.5 m cream Thai silk
- bolster insert (Spotlight)
- stencil pattern of your choice, stencil brush, gold fabric paint
- 3 m Mokuba 4546 col. 12 (cream), 15 mm wide
- 3 m Mokuba 1505 col. 14 (gold), 15 mm wide
- 3 m Mokuba 4597 col. 14 (gold stripe organdy), 15 mm wide
- cream Madeira floss
- gold Glista thread
- 3 m pure silk ribbon col. 56 (lime green), 4 mm wide
- DMC ecru
- 2 m cream cord
- 1 m gold braid
- 2 large cream tassels

Method

1   Determine your material requirements by measuring it over the bolster shape and cut to size.

2   Stencil your chosen design on each end of the fabric.

3   Make four cream ribbon roses for each end and stitch in place in centre of pattern. Embroider ribbon buds using gold rayon ribbon around each rose as shown. Embroider reverse ribbon leaves on each rose in gold stripe organdy ribbon.

4   Embroider straight stitch buds using cream floss and add Glista thread as fly stitch around each bud. Embroider lazy daisy leaves in Glista also around groups of buds. Embroider lazy daisy leaves in pure silk lime green ribbon where shown on gold buds.

5   Using DMC ecru in three strands, embroider stem stitch along stencil pattern as shown. Embroider Glista gold thread over DMC ecru to create a rope effect and add bullion stitches and long straight stitches to resemble tassels. Embroider gold bullions with lazy daisy leaves either side as shown.

6   Stitch cream cord either side of stencil pattern and gold braid on inside of cream cord as shown.

7   Make up bolster cushion adding cream tassels to either end.

Above: template for Formal Glory bolster at 50%.

Cameo Cherub

One of the fabulous areas of embroidery is being able to include all manner of objects in your design. I found this delicate cherub in a giftware shop and combined it in an embroidery of soft billowing ribbons and garlands of roses where the effect looks totally romantic.

Materials

- 50 cm x 80 cm turquoise Thai silk
- 50 cm x 50 cm gold mesh silk organza
- 1 m Mokuba 4547 organdy col. 8 (turquoise), 25 mm wide
- 1 m Mokuba 2500 velvet col. 44 (turquoise), 25 mm wide
- 1 m Mokuba pink and green flower braid
- 1 m Mokuba 4546 col. 29 (dusky pink organdy), 15 mm wide
- 1 m Mokuba 4546 col. 31 (pink organdy), 15 mm wide
- 2 m Mokuba 4544 col. 29 (dusky pink organdy), 25 mm wide
- 1 m dusky pink double-sided satin ribbon, 8 mm wide
- 2 m pale green rayon ribbon, 15 mm wide
- 4 m pure silk ribbon col. 162 (pale pink), 4 mm wide
- DMC 3727 (pink)
- DMC 225 (pale pink)
- DMC 966 (green), 1 strand
- hand-painted cherub (from gift shops)
- strong tacky glue

Method

1   Join Thai silk and gold organza together with a few small stitches.

2   Make a bow with organdy ribbon and pleat softly stitching each pleat in position. Stitch velvet ribbon in same manner, pleating as you stitch. Weave pink and green flower braid around velvet ribbon and stitch in place.

3   Make small ribbon roses using satin and organdy ribbons and sew in clusters as shown.

4   Embroider reverse ribbon leaves in pale green ribbon.

5   Using pure silk pale pink ribbon embroider silk ribbon buds with bullion stitches in DMC pinks (two strands) trailing from them. Attach buds with one strand of DMC green and embroider lazy daisy leaves with the same DMC green thread.

6   Glue cherub in position with a strong tacky glue.

7   My framer has used some of the leftover Thai silk and covered the oval mount. I glued some old lace and four dusky pink bows using Mokuba wide pink organdy ribbon in each corner to create a very three-dimensional look.

Above: template for Cameo Cherub at 55%.

Hydrangea Bon Bon

Whenever I pick flowers from my garden or purchase some of the more exquisite varieties available, I always tend to imagine them as an embroidery. By matching threads and ribbons to the colours of your blooms, you can begin to create a stilllife in embroidery and a lasting impression of the colours embraced by nature.

The hydrangeas in my garden always remind me of my grandmother's garden — they are such an old-fashioned flower. I am always sorry when the last of the bright blooms disappear, so I decided to capture them in an embroidery.

I have never been an advocate for using embroidery hoops, as I find them awkward, but I think if you have always used one they can be of great benefit in making this type of embroidery easier.

Materials

- 1.5 m pale blue Thai silk for face of hydrangeas, ruche and back of cushion
- 53 cm x 43 cm (49 cm x 39 cm when made up) gold Thai silk shot with pale blue
- gold and green fabric paint
- wadding to pad hydrangeas
- 1 m fine gold cord for stitching around leaves

The following show colours used for each individual flower:

Pale Pink Hydrangea
- Madeira 0807 (pale mauve) 3 strands
- Anchor 090 (pink) 3 strands
- Semco 867 (pale lilac) 3 strands
- DMC flower thread 2316 (pink) 3 strands
- DMC 6113 (green) 2 strands, mixed with Madeira 0807 (pale mauve) 1 strand
- Centre: DMC flower thread 2316 (pink)
     DMC 746 (cream) 3 strands

Dark Pink Hydrangea
- DMC stranded 3042 (lavender) 2 strand ⎫
- DMC Perle 644 (grey/green) 1 strand ⎬ mixed together more green effect
- DMC flower thread 2719 (plum) 3 strands ⎭
- DMC flower thread 2724 (deep plum) 3 strands
- DMC stranded 3731 (coral) 3 strands
- DMC stranded 3607 (fuschia) 3 strands
- Centre: DMC stranded 834 (gold) 3 strands

Blue Hydrangea
- DMC stranded 3755 (vivid blue) 3 strands
- DMC stranded 3746 (French blue) 3 strands
- DMC stranded 809 (blue) 3 strands
- DMC stranded 6113 (pale green) 2 strands ⎫ mixed together more green
- DMC stranded 775 (pale blue) 1 strand ⎭ effect
- DMC stranded 6113 (pale green) 1 strand ⎫ mixed together more blue
- DMC stranded 775 (pale blue) 2 strand ⎭ effect
- Centre: DMC stranded 834 (gold) 3 strands - 1 wrap
     DMC stranded 775 (pale blue) 3 strands - 3 wraps

Bee
- ◆   DMC stranded 3021 (dark brown) 1 strand
- ◆   DMC stranded 3046 (light gold) 1 strand
- ◆   DMC stranded 783 (light tan) 1 strand

Leaves
- ◆   DMC Perle 644 (light green)
- ◆   DMC stranded 3012 (green)

Method

1   The hydrangeas are first embroidered on pale blue silk and later appliqued onto the gold silk.

2   Follow the colour groupings set out in *Materials* above, and embroider each set of flowers using the *Techniques and Stitch Glossary* as a guide, and remembering to combine those colours stated for a shaded effect.

3   Scatter French knots randomly through each group, using the colours stated.

4   Draw leaf shapes around hydrangeas and paint a wash of green and gold paint to add depth. Allow to dry.

5   Embroider the leaf shapes in stem stitch using DMC Perle green around the edges and along the veins. The shaded areas of leaf are worked in stem stitch with two strands DMC 3012 (green).

6   The bee is embroidered in one strand only. Work body in straight vertical stitches using 3021 (dark brown), 3046 (light gold) and 783 (light tan) alternatively to form stripes. Wings are embroidered in lazy daisy stitches using 3021 (dark brown) and 3046 (light gold).

7   Cut small shapes of wadding to fit behind each hydrangea and stitch lightly in place.

8   Cut around leaves and hydrangeas leaving 1 cm for seam. Fold seam under and stitch in place using a fine running stitch.

9   Applique hydrangeas to gold silk and sew gold cord around some of the leaves as shown in the photograph.

10   Make up cushion with 5 cm ruche at either end to resemble a Bon Bon.

Above: template for Hydrangea Bon Bon at 65%

Techniques and Stitch Glossary

Step 1

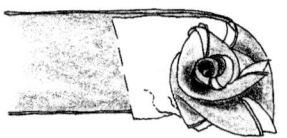

Step 13

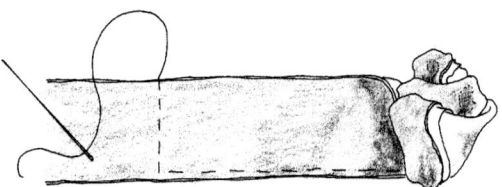

Step 14

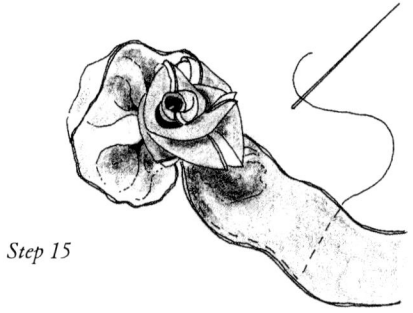

Step 15

Iceberg Rose

Step 1
Combine wire-edged and satin ribbon and then follow the instructions for Ribbon Rose, beginning on page 69.

Step 13
Continue by cutting off only the satin ribbon, and secure at the flower base.

Step 14
Make a gathering stitch along a 5 cm length at the base of the wire-edged ribbon, then stitch across the ribbon at right angles to the selvedges.

Step 15
Pull tightly to form gathered petal, stitch securely at the base of the rose.

Step 16
Repeat steps 14 and 15 five times to create six petals. Cut off excess ribbon and secure to the base of the rose. Secure the rose to the design with stitches through folds of the central rose.

Tip: *if rose becomes mis-shapen, bend the wire to the desired shape.*

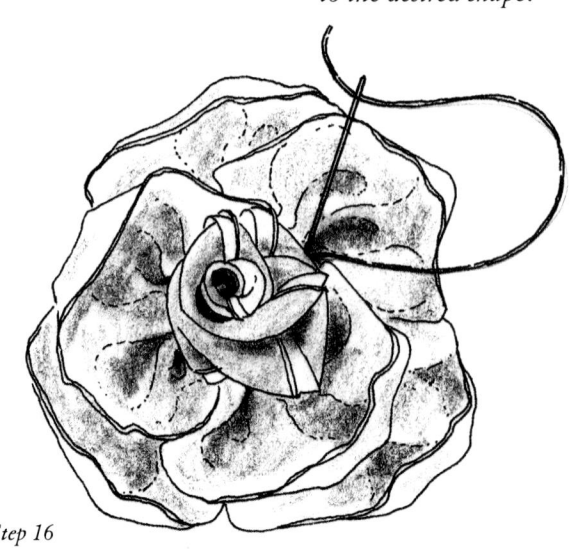

Step 16

French Rose

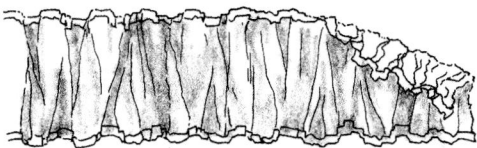

Step 1

Step 1
Using crinkle ribbon — fold top edge in.

Step 2
Fold raw edge in 1 cm.

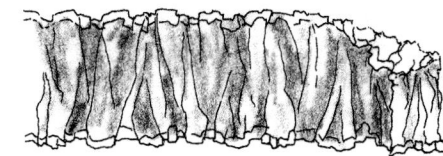

Step 2

Step 3
Roll loosely twelve times. Secure at base, making sure to include all ribbon folds.

Step 4
Fold ribbon away from roll at right angles.

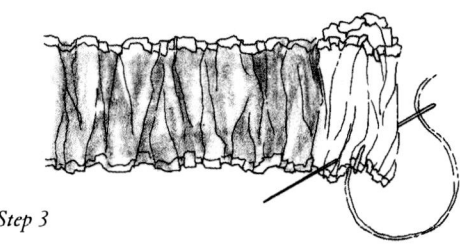

Step 3

Step 5
Roll flower bud one full rotation toward ribbon length.

Step 6
Repeat step 4, then roll flower bud toward ribbon length one half rotation. Repeat this three times.

Step 7
Stitch left and right sides of bud, making sure ALL ribbon folds are secured. Cut ribbon length 4 cm from bud, fold ribbon end under and secure at base of rose.

Step 4

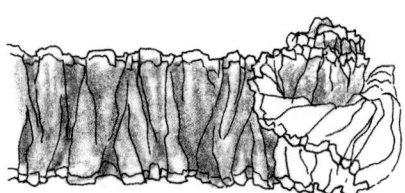

Step 5

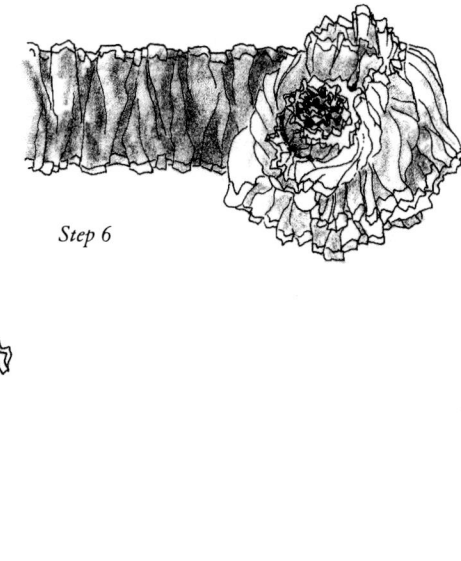

Step 6

Step 7

Step 8

Step 8
Secure smooth satin-edged ribbon at base of bud.

Step 9
Make a running stitch along base of ribbon for 18 cm.

Step 10
Gather ribbon and secure at the base of the rose to form a frilled petal.

Step 11
Repeat steps 9 and 10 another four times to create five petals. Cut off excess ribbon and secure neatly at base of rose.

Step 9

Step 10

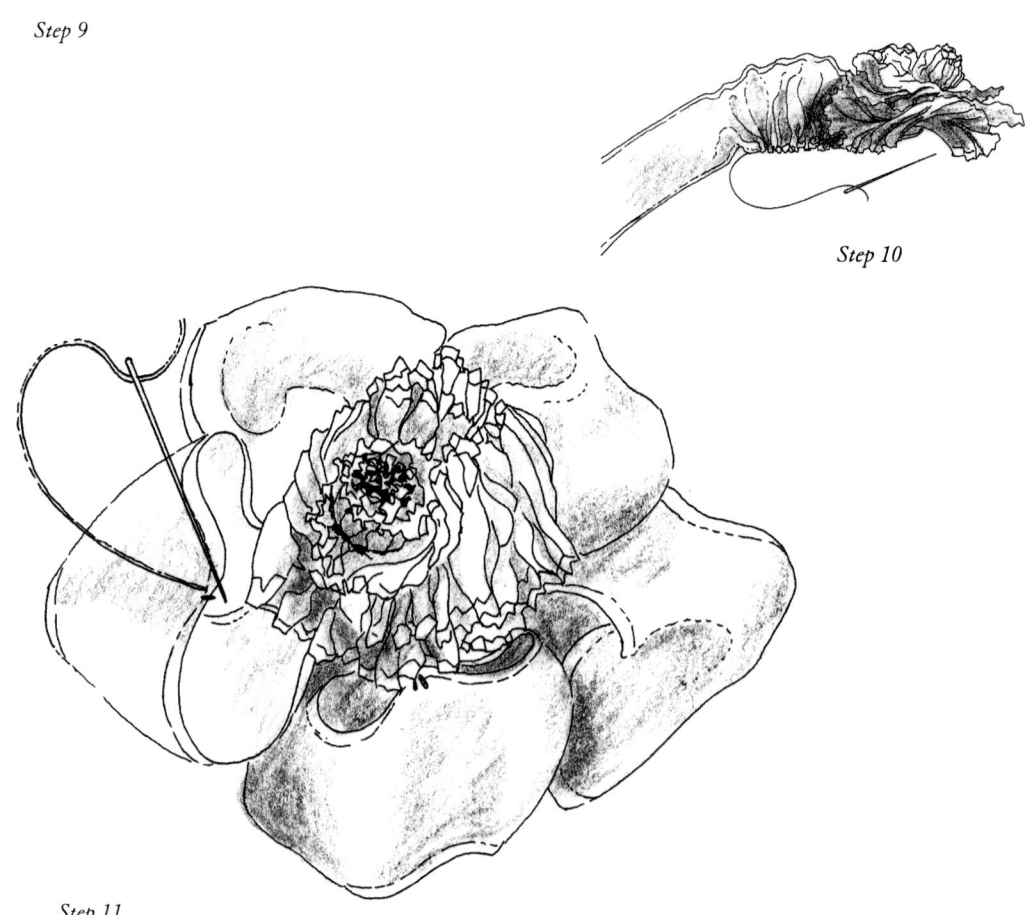

Step 11

Ribbon Rose

Step 1
Fold edge of ribbon over at corner.

Step 2
Roll end of ribbon several times to cover folded edge.

Step 3
Stitch securely one-third of the way up this roll.

Step 4
Stitch several times to ensure the coil does not unfold.

Step 5
Turn top of ribbon away from roll as shown.

Step 6
Roll the central roll toward the turned away ribbon (to the left) and stitch left side and base securely.

Step 7
Stitch right side and base several times. This will ensure rose will not fall apart.

Step 1

Step 2

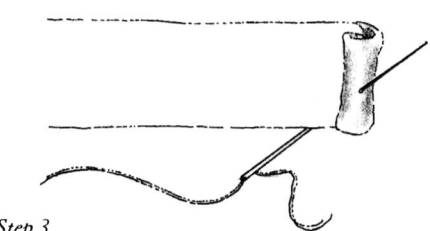

Step 3

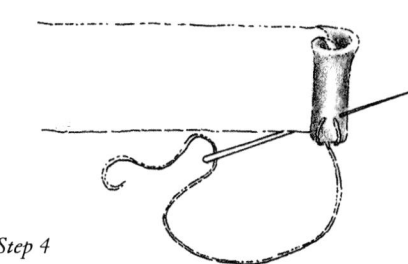

Step 4

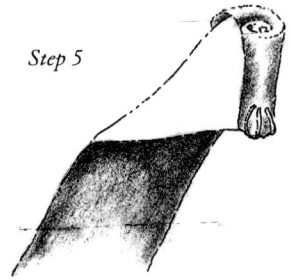

Step 5

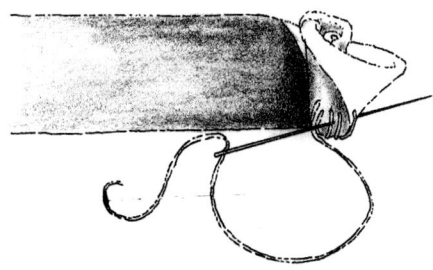

Step 6

Step 7

Step 8

Step 8
Turn left ribbon length away from central bud, as shown.

Step 9
Roll ribbon bud onto folded length.

Step 9

Step 10
Stitch securely at base and sides as shown.

Step 11
These steps are repeated, as shown, until you achieve the desired size of the rose.

Step 12
Cut ribbon and stitch at base of the rose, tucking in corners and raw edges.

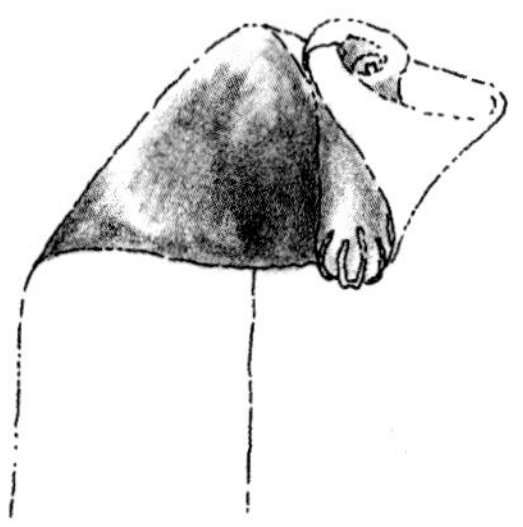

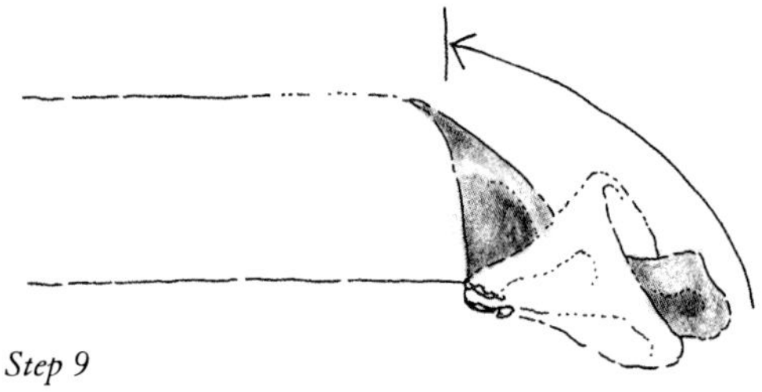

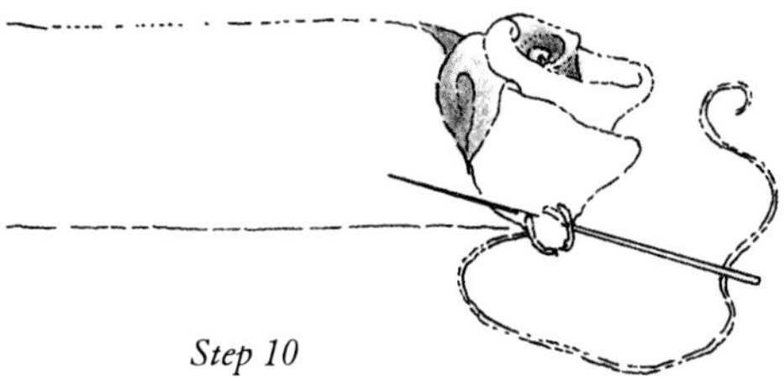

Step 10

Step 11

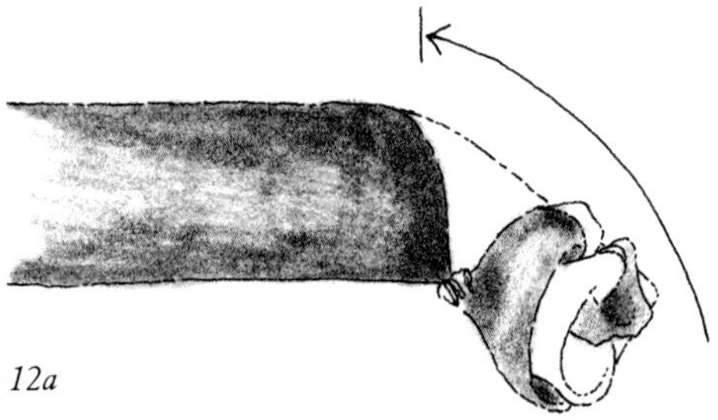

Step 12a

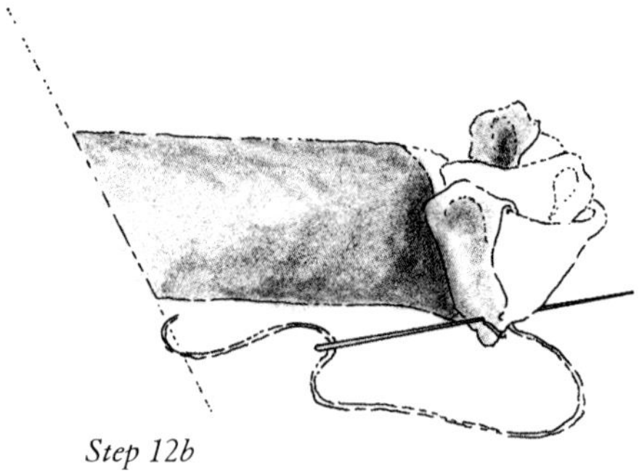

Step 12b

Step 12c

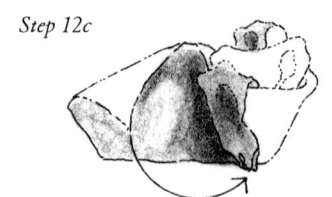

Tea Rose

Make as per the Ribbon Rose Steps 1-12, then:

Step 13
Continue to make a tea rose.

Steps 14 and 15
See illustration

Step 16
Using left hand, loop ribbon length as shown.

Step 17
Stitch to secure at the base of the rose.

Step 18
Loop ribbon on other side of first loop and stitch again at the base of the rose.

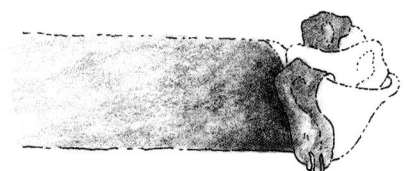

Step 13

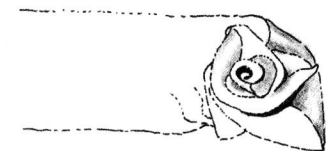

Step 14

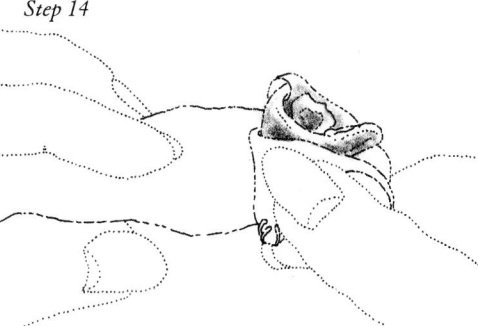

Step 15

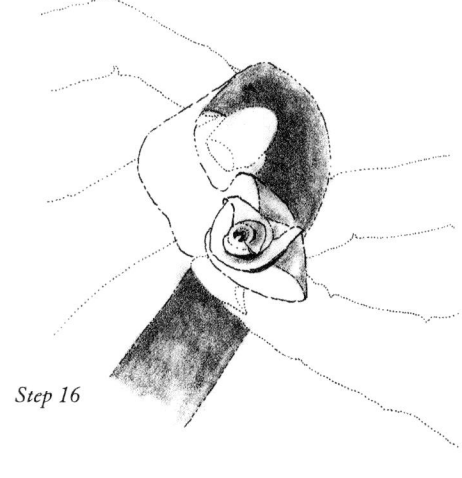

Step 16

Step 17

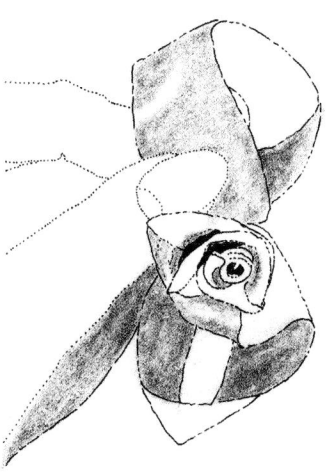

Step 18

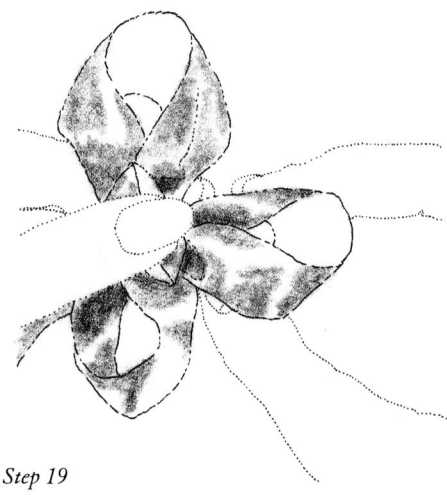

Step 19

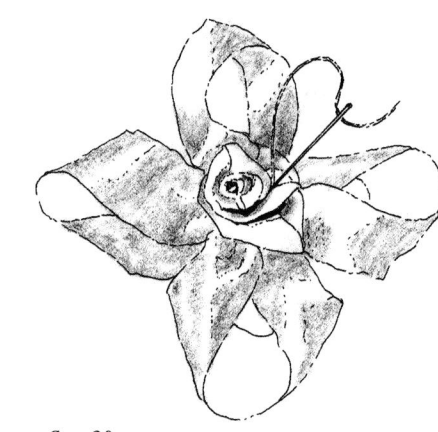

Step 20

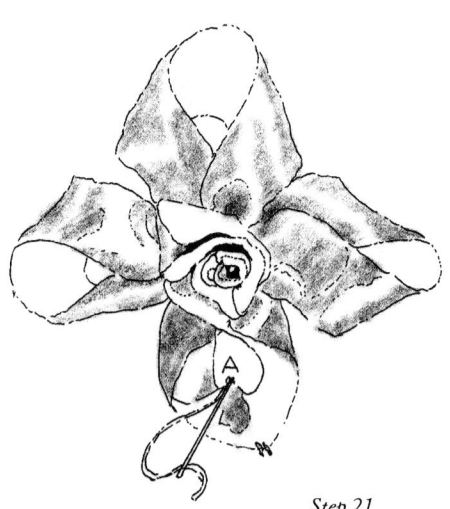

Step 21

Step 19

Continue to loop ribbon length as shown and stitch securely. You can make the tea roses larger or more full by repeating these steps in between the petals already made.

Step 20

When rose is at desired size cut off excess ribbon, fold cut edge over the back of the rose and stitch securely to hide the raw edge. To stitch rose to design, secure the centre of the rose by bringing needle up in the centre rose folds and stitch in place securely, in several places.

The outer petals may be manipulated into the desired shape, by using a needle and thread to secure them into different positions. The following demonstrates one method, but you can experiment with others.

Step 21

Bring the needle up under the centre point of each outer petal (working on one petal at a time). Using the tip of the needle, pierce the centre lower edge of the ribbon and secure. On the same petal, bring the needle up between the centre of the petal through the base fabric at point 'A'. Then pierce the centre of the top edge of the ribbon and return the needle through the fabric near 'A'.

Step 22

This method gives a soft rounded petal. Repeat Step 21 on all petals.

Step 22

Ribbon Bud (or Ribbon Leaf)

Step 1
Fold edge of ribbon over at right angles leaving a small seam allowance.

Step 2
Fold length of ribbon in toward first fold, slightly overlapping at the lower edge.

Step 3
Secure at base with a running thread, cut excess ribbon.

Step 4
Gently flatten ribbon to form leaf or bud.

Step 1

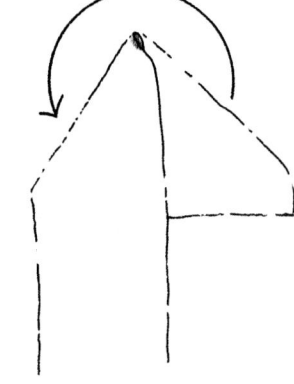

Step 2

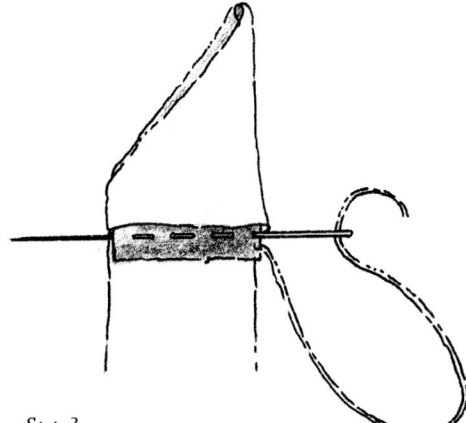

Step 3

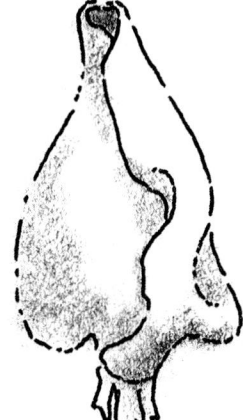

Step 4

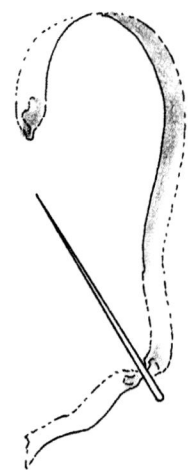

Step 1

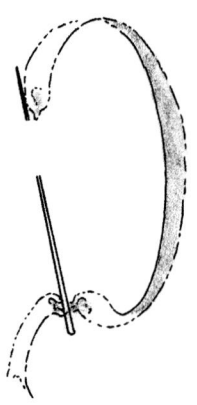

Step 2

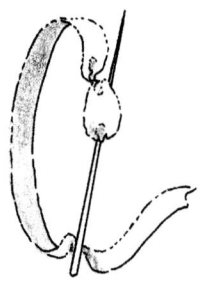

Step 3

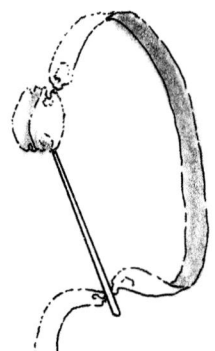

Step 4

Silk Ribbon Bud

Step 1
Enter the design at the top point of the bud, exit at the base of bud to desired height.

Step 2
Guide needle point slightly to the left of the top of the bud, gently draw through, taking care to keep the ribbon straight.

Step 3
Re-enter at the base of the bud and guide the needle point slightly to the right of the top of the bud; gently draw through, taking care to keep the ribbon straight.

Step 4
Re-enter at the base of the bud — finish the bud off on the reverse of work (secure with thread).

Step 5
To create bud leaves (Lazy Daisy Stitch). Taking an appropriate thread, pull up through the centre of the bud and ddown to the flower's base, draw through gently.

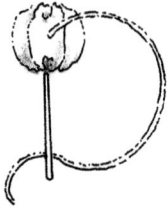

Step 5

Step 6
Re-enter near the base, but to the left of the bud.

Step 7
Guide the needle in beside the point where the thread comes up (Step 6), and out at the point to the left of the bud which will determine the length of the leaf, ensuring that the loop formed by the thread is caught under the needle.

Step 8
Re-enter the cloth on the far side of the loop to secure the leaf in place.

Step 9
Construct a second leaf on the right of the bud in the same manner as the first leaf.

Step 10
Bring the needle up through the cloth at the base of the bud, re-enter at the point to make the desired stem length.

Step 11
Secure at the reverse of the design: finished Silk Ribbon Bud.

Step 6

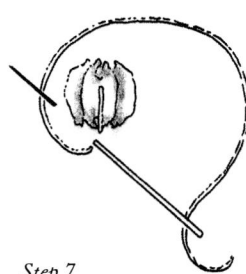

Step 7

Step 8

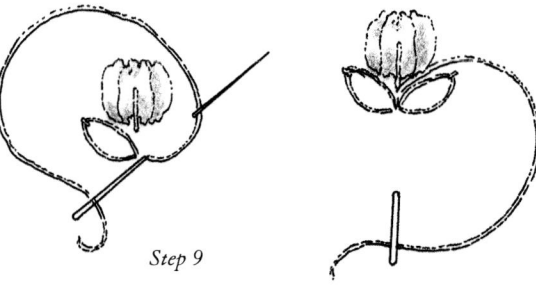

Step 9

Step 10

Step 11

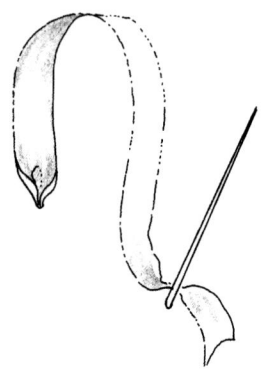

Step 1

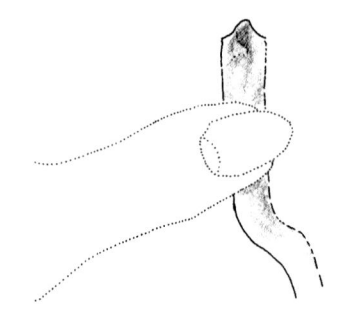

Step 2

Reverse Ribbon Leaf

Step 1
Pull needle and ribbon up to the front of the work at the point where the leaf is to be placed.

Step 2
Draw ribbon down, with right side facing, hold in place with the left thumb.

Step 3
Still holding the ribbon in place with the thumb, insert the needle into the ribbon and through the base cloth.

Step 4
Draw ribbon through carefully, ensuring ribbon does not twist.

Step 5
When ribbon is pulled through, trim and secure at the back of the work.

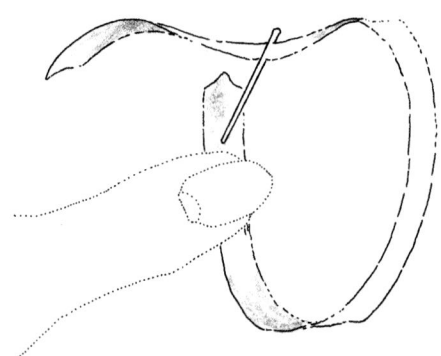

Step 3

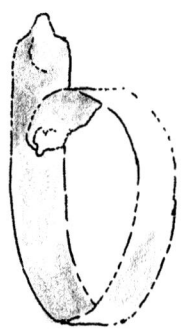

Step 4

Step 5

Straight Stitch Bud

Make as per the Silk Ribbon Bud Steps 1-4, then:

Step 5
Using a finer material than that of which the Buds are made — from the back of the base cloth enter the design to the left and halfway up the height of the bud. Re-enter at the same point on the right of the bud, this time from the face of the cloth. Bring the point of the needle up at the base of the bud and be sure that the needle passes over the top of the loop created by the thread.

Step 6
Pull through gently. The loop will be caught by the thread and create the 'V' at the base of bud. Re-enter the cloth at the point which will create the desired length of the bud's stem. Secure at the reverse of the design.

Step 7
Finished Straight Stitch Bud.

Step 5

Step 6

Step 7

Scabiosa

Note: best results for this flower are achieved with a wide ribbon.

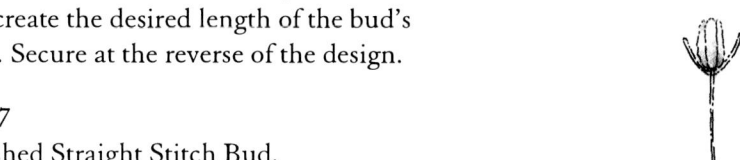

Step 1

Step 1
Make a Gathering stitch as illustrated across the raw edge of the ribbon to anchor. Continue to gather along the edge of the ribbon length for about 5 cm before gathering across the ribbon as shown. Repeat each section five times.

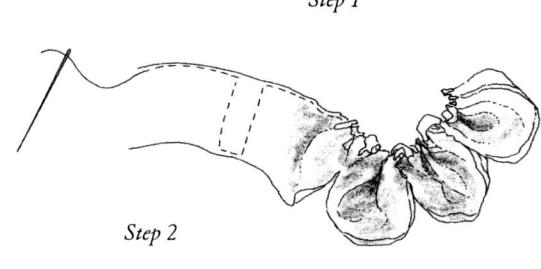

Step 2

Step 2
Draw thread tightly to form a Scabiosa.

Step 3
Cut excess ribbon. Sew raw edges to the back of the flower.

Step 3

Step 1

Step 2

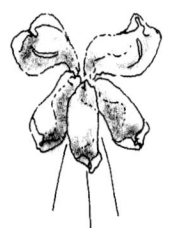

Step 3

Step 4

Silk Ribbon Fuschia

Step 1
Embroider three long Reverse Ribbon stitches to form 'skirt' of flower.

Step 2
Using a slightly wider ribbon, work two shorter Reverse Ribbon stitches to create flower leaves.

Step 3
Place three Straight stitches from the 'skirt' to form the stamens.

Step 4
At the end of each stamen embroider a French Knot and sew a single Long stitch from the centre of the flower to create the stem.

Ribbon Fuschia

Step 1
Fold edge of ribbon over at corner.

Step 2
Roll end of the ribbon several times to cover folded edge.

Step 3
Create four pleats along ribbon length.

Step 1

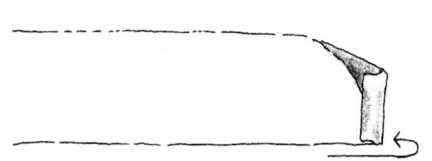

Step 2

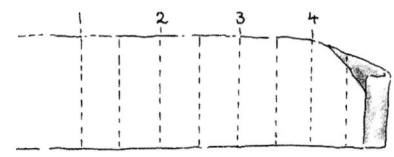

Step 3

78

Step 4
Draw all pleats evenly on top of the ribbon roll created in Step 2.

Step 5
Secure all folds at flower base.

Step 6
Bring ribbon length around in front of the existing petal, pinch and secure at base. Cut off excess ribbon.

Step 7
Work two twisted Reverse Ribbon leaves to form the flower's calyx.

Step 8
Embroider stamen by combining one Straight stitch and a Straight stitch bud.

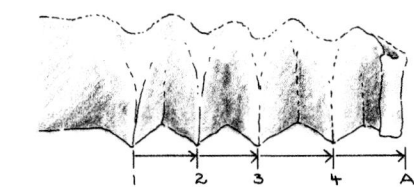

Step 4

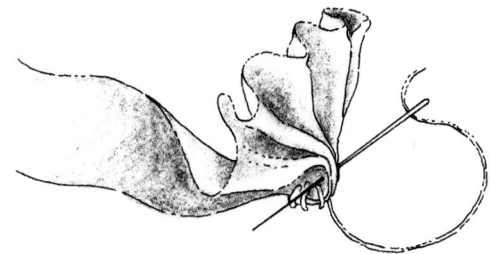

Step 5

Step 6

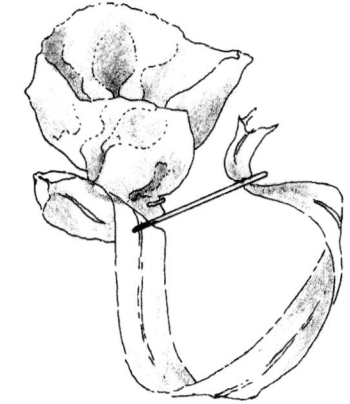

Step 7

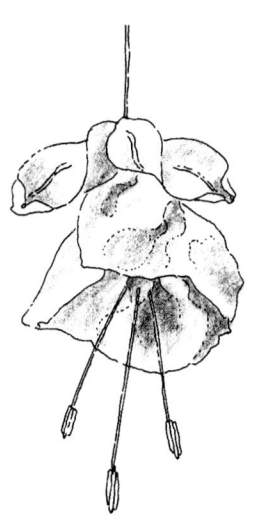

Step 8

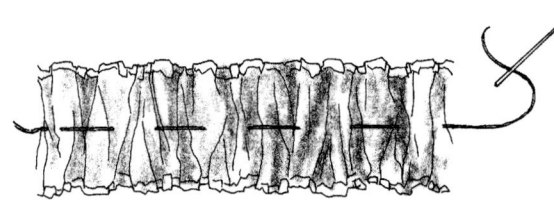

Step 1

Step 2

Step 3

Step 4

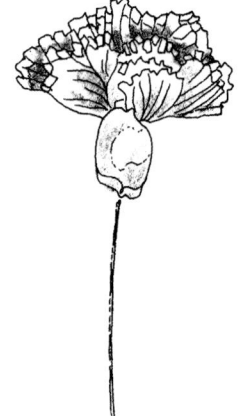

Step 5

Carnation

Step 1

Using crinkle ribbon, run large Gathering stitches along the centre of a length of ribbon approximately 20 cm long.

Step 2

Draw in tightly and cut excess ribbon.

Step 3

Stitch the corner of the two raw edges of the ribbon on the flower face and secure to centre of the flower. Repeat on the back of the flower.

Step 4

For a half carnation — gather 8 cm of ribbon in the same manner as for the large carnation. Fold flower in half, stitch through at the base to hold.

Step 5

Secure to the fabric keeping the ribbon pressed flat as you attach it. Add one Reverse Ribbon Leaf to base of flower to create the calyx.

Flannel Flower

Step 1

Embroider four Reverse Ribbon Leaves at right angles (for the half flower use three leaves) to each other to form a circle.

Step 2

Place an additional Reverse Ribbon Leaf between each of the four leaves. Using Floss or thread, fill in the centre of the flower with Straight stitches.

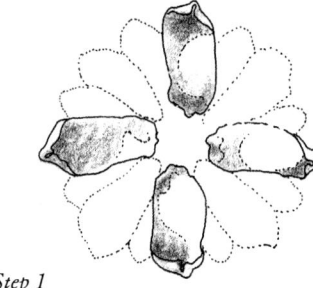

Step 1

Step 2

Step 3
Finished flower.

Step 3

Wisteria

Step 1
Follow the instructions on how to create a Silk Ribbon bud up to step 4 — embroidering four medium-sized and two small silk buds as shown here.

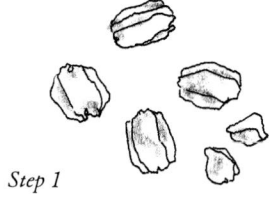

Step 1

Step 2
On either side of the silk buds work a Straight stitch bud.

Step 3
Create approximately five Straight Stitches in each bud. Above the two smaller silk buds sew two small Straight stitch buds made up of three individual Straight stitch buds. Vary the colour of the central bud.

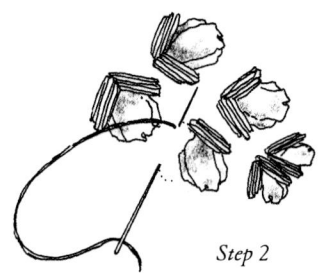

Step 2

Step 4
Place single, elongated bullion stitches around the central flowers in the pattern.

Step 5
Coil the thread twenty times around the needle to create the elongated stitch.

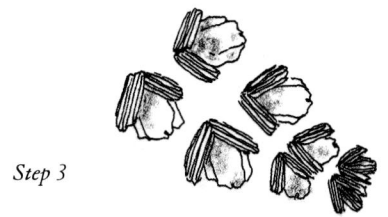

Step 3

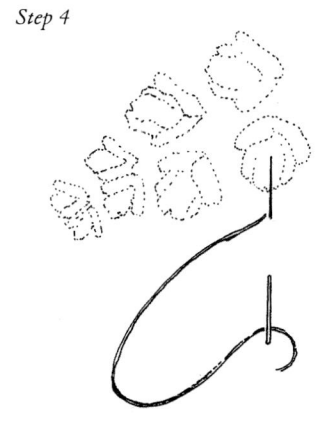

Step 4

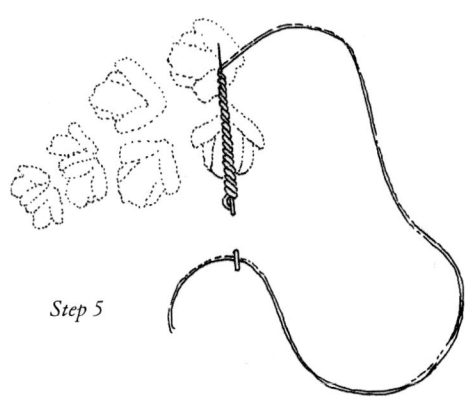

Step 5

Step 6

Step 6
Secure bullion stitch into position and continue to place them as illustrated.

Step 7
Bullion stitches in place.

Step 8
Position Straight stitch stems as indicated.

Step 7

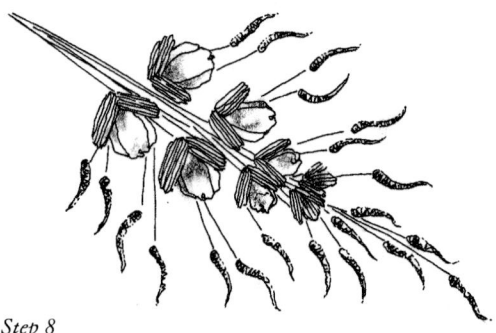

Step 8

Chrysanthemum

Step 1
Loosely twirl ribbon.

Step 1

Step 2
Bring needle down into ribbon at required petal length — gently pull through.

Step 3
Do not pull tightly as the curly effect requires the ribbon to be loose.

Step 4
Repeat this process four or five times on each side of the flower as shown, varying the length of each petal to create the flower shape.

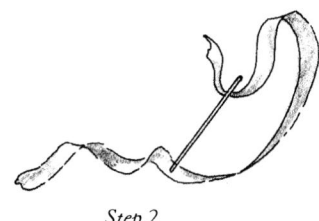

Step 2

Step 3

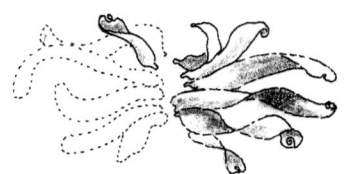

Step 4

Step 5
Embroider several (six to eight) Straight stitches at the top of the flower to create stamens.

Step 6
Embroider a French Knot at the top of each stamen.

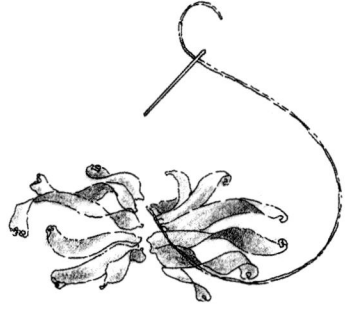

Step 5

Step 6

Bluebells

Step 1
Place five ribbon Straight stitches to form this Silk Ribbon bud as the basis of the Bluebell.

Step 2
Four long silk ribbon Straight stitches create the flower's petals.

Step 3
Using white Floss, embroider three Straight stitches to form stamens.

Step 4
Work one long Straight stitch for stem.

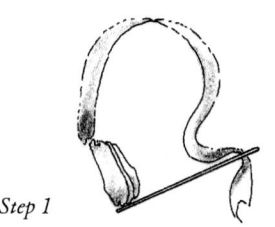

Step 1

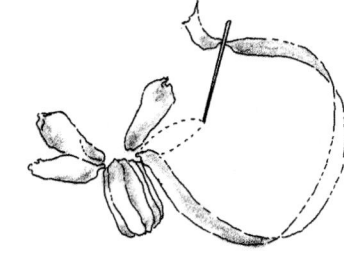

Step 2

Step 3

Step 4

83

Queen Anne Lace

Step 1
Embroider two slightly angled Straight stitches.

Step 2
Add remaining stitches as shown.

Step 3
Embroider small white French Knots at the top of each stem.

Step 4
Create the stem with one long Straight stitch.

Step 1

Step 2

Step 3

Step 4

Camellia Star-above-Star — White Flower

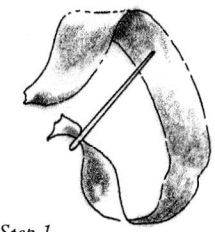

Step 1

Step 1
The White Flower is made in a similar way to Reverse Ribbon Leaf - only each petal is folded as shown.

Step 2
The first petal placed should be one of the top two petals.

Step 2

Step 3
Position the second petal close to and beside the first. Repeat until you have two or three pairs (depending upon the size of the flower required). Each pair should be placed directly beneath the other and overlapping slightly.

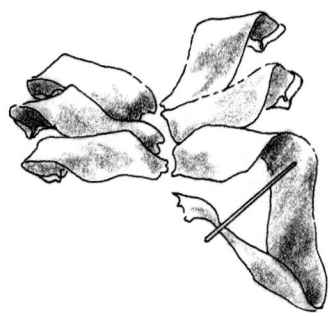

Step 3

Step 4
Embroider the centre bud with either Floss or fine silk ribbon to form either a large Straight stitch bud (of ten stitches) or a Silk Ribbon bud (of five stitches).

Step 5
Add two Reverse Ribbon Leaves at base of the flower. The stem is worked in Stem stitch.

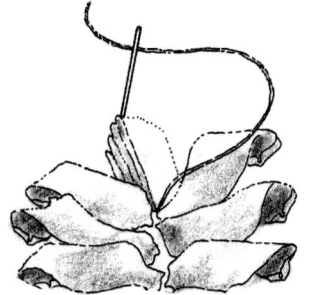

Step 4

Step 5

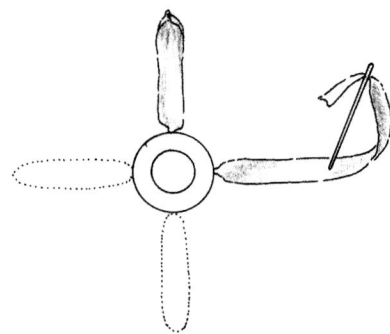

Step 1

Step 2

Step 3

Step 4

Gerbera

Step 1
Draw two circles on the fabric — one large circle with a smaller circle in the centre of the larger one. Work four Reverse Ribbon stitches at right angles around the outer circle.

Step 2
Fill in between the first four petals, varying the length of each petal a little as you work.

Step 3
Embroider Straight stitches from the edge of the central circle to the outer circle and fill in.

Step 4
At the edge of the outer circle embroider French Knots. Fill the central circle with French Knots and create a stem by laying silk ribbon in place and working Stem stitch in thread down the centre.

Sweet Pea

Step 1
Fold edge of ribbon over at corner.

Step 2
Roll end of ribbon several times to cover folded edge.

Step 3 *(see illustration page 87)*
Stitch securely one-third of the way up this roll.

Step 1 — Sweet Pea

Step 2 — Sweet Pea

Step 4
Create four pleats butting up against the flower centre.

Step 5
Draw pleats over the top of each other and the flower centre. Secure at base.

Step 6
Gently open out the petal and continue to hold ...

Step 7
Bring ribbon around in front of the existing petal.

Step 8
Now, curve the ribbon to the flower base, pinch and secure.

Step 9
Sew the flower into position on the design. Hide the raw edges at the base with two Reverse Ribbon leaves.

Step 10
One strand of green thread is used in Stem stitch to embroider a tendril from the Sweet Pea.

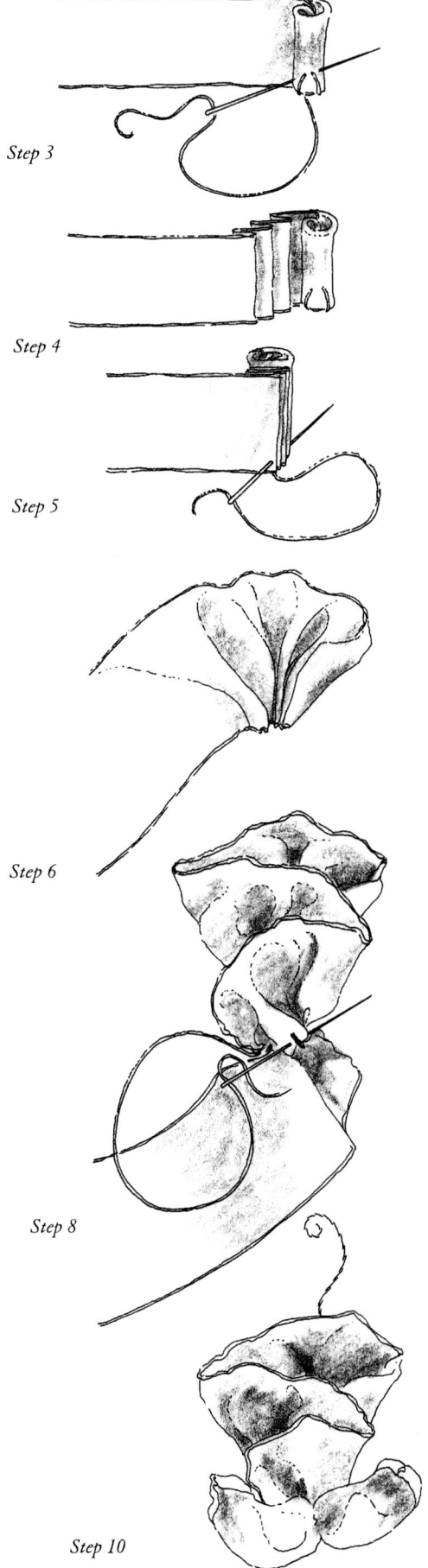

Step 3

Step 4

Step 5

Step 6

Step 8

Step 10

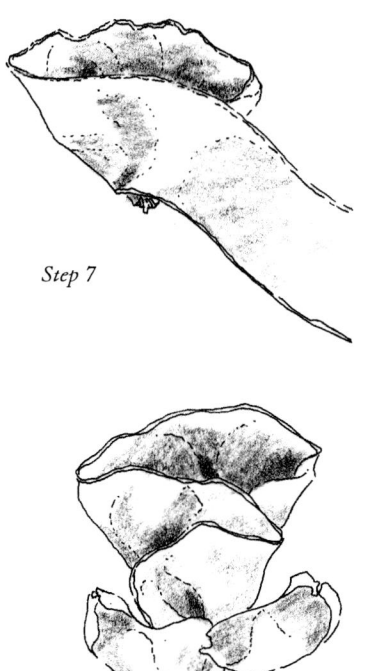

Step 7

Step 9

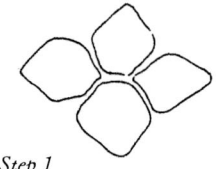

Step 1

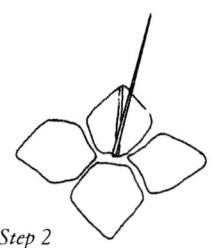

Step 2

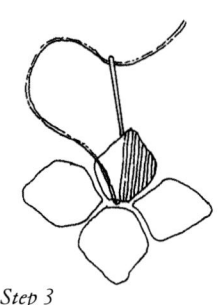

Step 3

Hydrangea

Step 1
Draw the shape of each flowerette on to the fabric in three large clusters. Each single flower is repeated to form a Hydrangea.

Step 2
Fill in each petal — working from the centre out to one edge.

Step 3
Continue on the other side of the petal.

Step 4
Work each flower in the same manner changing shades as required.

Step 5
Each petal is outlined in Stem stitch. Begin at the base of each individual petal.

Step 6
Use one strand of thread in Stem stitch to outline the petals.

Step 7
Embroider one or more French Knots in the centre of each single flowerette.

Step 4

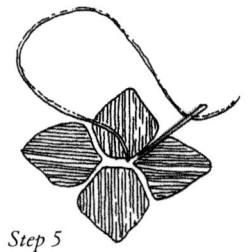

Step 5

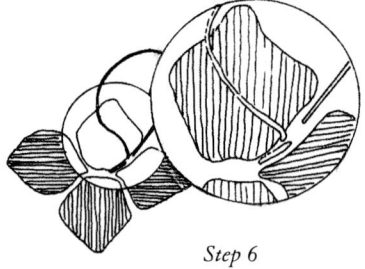

Step 6

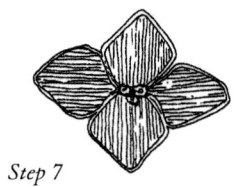

Step 7

Split Buds

Step 1

Step 1
Embroider two Straight stitch buds of three stitches each as shown.

Step 2

Step 2
Sew two single thread Straight stitches to form stamens.

Step 3
Stem of flower is a single Straight stitch thread.

Step 3

Star Flower

Step 1
Embroider four Straight stitches at right angles to each other.

Step 1

Step 2
Work around the flower design, placing the remaining stitches evenly to create the flower.

Step 2

Step 3
Vary the stitch length for a more natural look.

Step 4
At flower's centre embroider three French Knots.

Step 3

Step 4

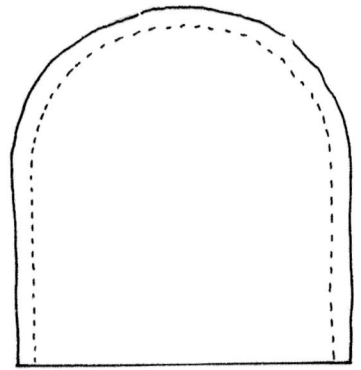

Step 1

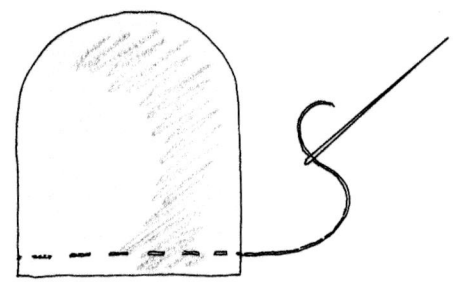

Step 2

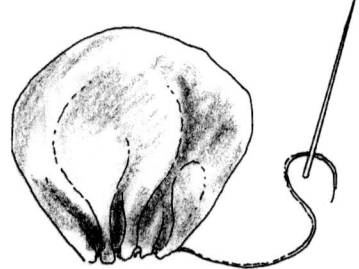

Step 3

Lily Pad Petal

Step 1
Double the cloth to cut both sides of the petal — both large or small sizes.

Step 2
With wrong sides together, sew a narrow seam around the edge of the petal, turn inside-out and press.

Step 3
At the base of the petal, sew a running stitch and draw tightly.

Step 4
Sew in place.

Satin Stitch

Step 1
Bring the needle and thread to the face of the fabric. Make a backward straight stitch at the edge of the shape to be 'coloured in'.

Step 2
Alongside this initial stitch, make another (keeping stitches close to each other).

Step 3
Continue working in this fashion.

Step 4
Continue until shape is completed.

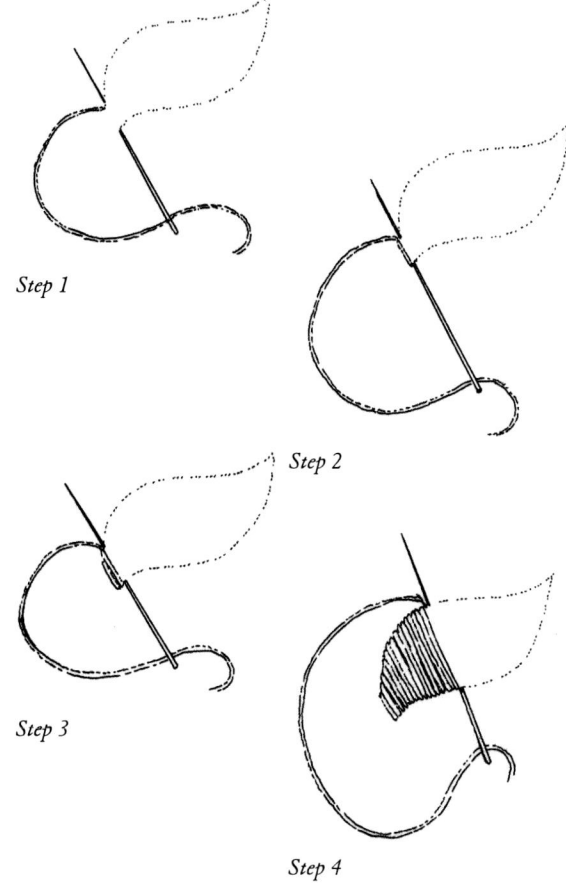

Step 1

Step 2

Step 3

Step 4

French Knot

Step 1
Start with thread and needle pulled through to the face of the fabric (point A). Wind the thread around the needle and return the needle into the fabric just beside point A.

Step 2
Gently pull thread through loop and fabric to back of cloth.

Step 3
Secure at the back of the cloth — finished knot.

Step 4
For a lrager knot, wind the thread around the needle a couple of times. Re-enter at point A.

Step 5
Gently push the needle and thread through to the back of the fabric.

Step 6
Secure at the back of the fabric: finished knot.

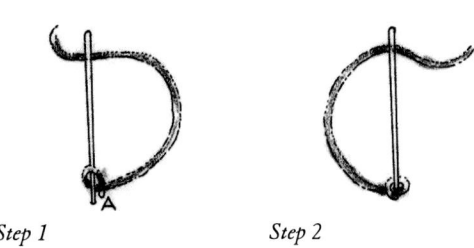

Step 1   *Step 2*

Step 3

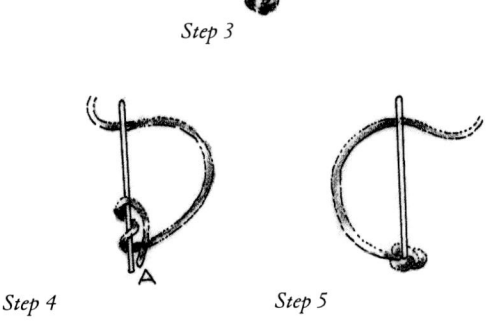

Step 4   *Step 5*

Step 6

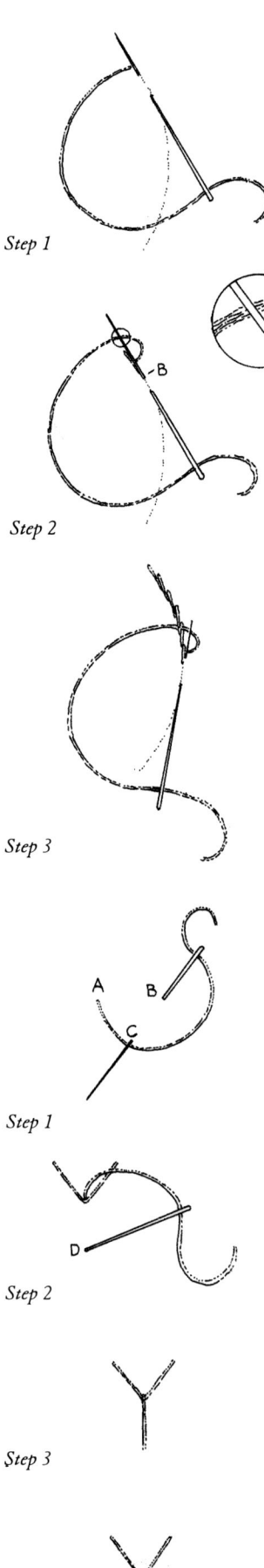

Step 1

Step 2

Step 3

Step 1

Step 2

Step 3

Step 4

Stem Stitch

Step 1
Bring the needle and thread up at the beginning of the line or outline. Keep the needle pointing away from the direction you are working. Make one large stitch back and guide the tip of the needle to the point halfway along this stitch.

Step 2
Make sure that the thread is under the point of the needle (see inset illustration). Pull through. Make another backward stitch half the size of the first stitch, bring the tip of the needle up along point B, but not into point B.

Step 3
Continue in this manner until you have completed the stem or outline.

Fly Stitch

Step 1
Bring the needle and thread up at point A. Insert needle at point B and guide tip of needle to point C. Make sure that the needle passes over the loop created.

Step 2
Bring the needle and thread over the V shape created, re-enter fabric at point D.

Step 3
This creates a Y shape ideal for smaller flowers.

Step 4
Or, alternatively, make a very short stem, thus making only a V shape.

Lazy Daisy Stitch

Step 1
Bring the needle and thread up to the face of the cloth. Create a loop, bring the needle back to the entry point, guiding the tip of the needle to the outer tip of the petal and through. Make sure that the needle passes over the thread (loop).

Step 2
Pull the needle and thread through. Make a tiny straight stitch over the tip of the petal, catching and securing the loop as you go.

Step 3
Repeat steps 1 and 2 around the flower for a simple daisy look.

Bullion Stitch

Step 1
Make a backstitch in the centre of the points A and B to secure the bullion stitch. Start stitch with thread on the right side of the fabric, insert the needle at the point for the desired stitch length (B); guide tip up at point A. Pull needle through until just the eye of the needle is showing: do not pull the thread through.

Step 2
Wind the thread clockwise around the needle, making sure that the first wrap is close to the base of the needle shaft. Do not cross the thread while wrapping — wrap the thread loosely.

Step 1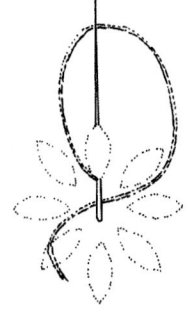

Step 2

Step 3

Step 1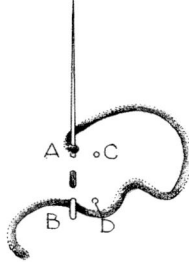

Step 2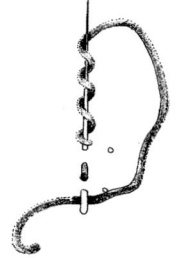

Step 3

Step 4

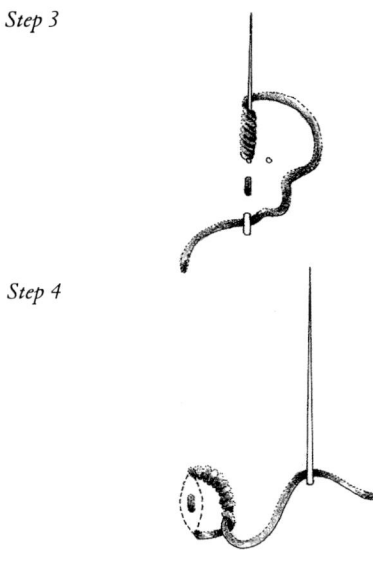

Step 5

Step 3
Wind until length of would thread on the needle will cover the desired length of the stitch (making allowance for the thread to compact when pulled through).

Step 4
Place the left thumb over the loose coil on the needle, then gently pull the needle and thread through. Keep the thumb on the bullion as it eases forward into position.

Step 5
To secure the stitch, place the needle just beside (but not in) point B, then guide the needle tip up at point C to start the second stitch to the right of the first.

Stockists

Victoria

Nancraft
370 Little Bourke Street
Melbourne Vic. 3000
03) 9670 6221

Horizon Fabrics
186 York Street
South Melbourne Vic. 3205
03) 9690 6867
(upholstery damask and fabrics)

Designer Trim
134 Bridge Road
Richmond Vic. 3121
03) 9428 5484

Robbyn Macdonald Embroidery
60 North Road
Brighton Vic. 3186
03) 9596 6514
(silk pictures, kits)

A Macdougall Pty Ltd
9 Cremorne Street
Richmond Vic. 3121
03) 9429 8038
(specialist ribbons, trimmings)

Attic Crafts
98 Queen Street
Bendigo Vic. 3550
054) 41 7333

E C Birch Pty Ltd
153 Bridge Road
Richmond Vic. 3121
03) 9429 4944
(all haberdashery needs)

Durrant-Ross Gallery and
Picture Framing
71 Durrant Street
Brighton Vic. 3186
03) 9592 4442
(specialist framers)

The Button Shop
181 Glenferrie Road
Malvern Vic. 3144
03) 9509 7077
(buttons, ribbons and braid
specialists)

The Embroidery Den
350b Bay Street
Brighton North Vic. 3186
03) 9596 5389
(all embroidery needs)

Lincraft
Australia on Collins
Collins Street
Melbourne Vic. 3000
03) 9650 1609

Old World Haberdashery
Chapel Street Bazaar
217-223 Chapel Street
Prahran Vic. 3181
03) 9529 1727
03) 9510 9841

Bustle and Bows
164 Union Road
Surrey Hills Vic. 3127
03) 9888 5018

New South Wales

The Embroidery Cupboard
150 Burnsbay Road
Lane Cove NSW 2066
02) 428 3049

Nerylla's Antiques
498 Miller Street
Cammeray NSW 2062
02) 9955 4230
(antique sewing collection)

Western Australia

Antique Rose
645 Beaufort Street
Mt Lawley WA 6050
09) 328 1779

Queensland

Gardams
63 Adelaide Street
Brisbane Qld 4000
03) 3221 4144

South Australia

Peejays Wool & Craft
Shop 25, Ingle Farm Shopping
Centre
Montague Road
Ingle Farm SA 5098

Acknowledgements

The creation of a book takes time and I am indebted to the following people for their assistance:

My wonderful husband Stuart, who has adapted so well to living with a creative mind and knew it was time to dust off the wok, and my two boys Lachlan and Taylor for just being gorgeous.

Dorothy Jurgens who is still a cushion-maker extraordinaire at 82. Her energy, kindness and positive attitude to life are an inspiration.

Alison Brewer for typing until 3.00 a.m. to finish my scrawled manuscript, and for being the best friend a girl could have.

Mokuba for providing me with such luxurious ribbons.

Lincraft for their help and assistance and use of their beautiful fabrics — and Katerina Dokolos for her enthusiasm and support.

Terry Gooding and Dale Conway from Durrant-Ross Gallery and Picture Framing whose expertise in framing speaks for itself, and for never saying no to one of my outlandish ideas.

Cristina Varasso from Flower Flower whose beautiful blooms adorn this book.

Custom Skylights for making the Perspex dome especially to fit Sweet Pea Fairy Dreams when everyone else said it couldn't be done.

Graham Lucas for his superb craftsmanship in upholstering my piano stool.

Janet Rowe for her invaluable advice and amazing patience.

Tony Quayle for his past support and care.

Hermine Miakian for her assistance with typing and looking after my family.

Bunty for being such a delightful little girl and beautiful fairy, and Anna from Fendi Hairdressing for creating 'fairy hair'.

Bryony Dade, once again, for her elaborate and beautifully drawn illustrations.

All my students who have become freinds and who continue to encourage and support me.

Neil Lorimer for his superb photography, his ability to transform corners of rooms into opulent settings, and his calm personality in the face of working two days with 'girl things'.

And finally, the old girl network — Alison Brewer, Gayle Cox, Val Ferguson, Liz Garratt, Glenys Richards, Helen and Louise Stanley, Thelma Wenke, Jan McGowan, Anita Murray and my friends at BGS.

Potpourri Friendship Quilt

I asked each woman for a small piece with the only requirement that it be worked on cream materials using pastel/dusky tones. I think the result is absolutely delightful and a lasting keepsake from friends. It is full of memories of embroidery classes as every piece reflects the individual personality and style of each woman.

Thanks to: Helen Stanley, Louise Stanley, Thelma Wenke, Alison Brewer, Debbie Male, Joyce Parkes, Lisa Gndy, Dianne Griffith, Michelle Duchini, Trisha Blance, Glenys Richards, Margaret Carolane, Julie Lambert, Katin Voyage, Toni Giannarelli, Valerie Ferguson, Paula Lane, Jan McGowan, Maria Kominos, Resie Alcott, Angela Parkes, Peggy Zervros, Avalene Puleo, Irene Kritkides, Lee Vautin, Kaye Carter, Michelle Kassavetis, Anita Murray, Anne Dutton, Peggy Paltos. (See photograph on page 4.)